Life is short.

Stop with the BS.

δ

START PUBLISHING

SAN FRANCISCO

STOP with the BS

SHANE MAC

START PUBLISHING

SAN FRANCISCO

Copyright © 2012 by Shane Mac

For information about permission to reproduce
selections from this book, write to Permissions, Start
Publishing, PO Box 2881, Sausalito, CA 94966

www.shanemac.me

ISBN-10: 0615645119
ISBN-13: 978-0615645117

Book Design by Sarah Kathleen Peck

Cover Design by Mike Rohde

To my mom, dad, brother, sister and best friends growing up.
I wrote this for you because of you. I love you.

CONTENTS

PROBABLY IN CALIFORNIA

SATURDAY

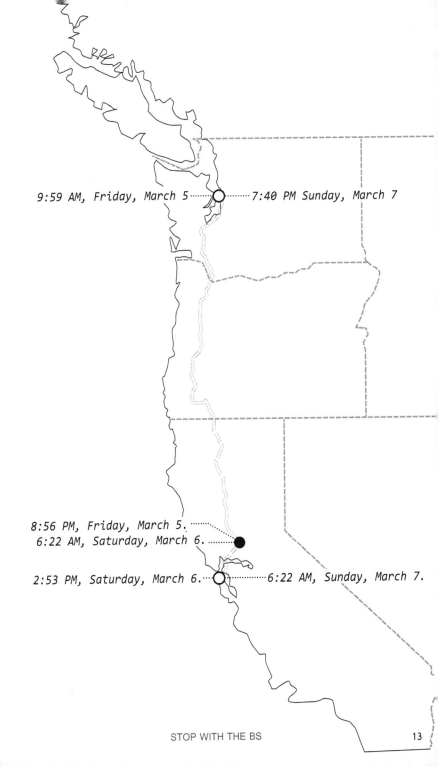

9:59 AM, Friday, March 5 ········O········ 7:40 PM Sunday, March 7

8:56 PM, Friday, March 5. ·······
6:22 AM, Saturday, March 6. ·······●

2:53 PM, Saturday, March 6. ·······O········ 6:22 AM, Sunday, March 7.

SHANE MAC

PREFACE

When I was in Seattle I decided to write a book. I didn't want to write "just another book"—since it seems like everyone and their brother has written a book these days—so I decided to try something different.

I have saved hundreds of thoughts over the years from my experience starting a company, becoming a professional musician, and working in a larger company which later was acquired.

I decided that I was going to write an entire book in 24 hours, on a train ride from Seattle to San Francisco and back. For each chapter, I took a picture out of the window and picked a different song to listen to. I also wrote in italics my real-time thoughts while writing the book. I wanted people to be there with me when they read this book.

This is (mostly) un-edited, un-designed, raw and real thoughts from two years ago. This is what I learned. I am still learning.

With love,

Shane Mac

Friday, March 5, 2010

9:59 AM

1:11 PM

LEAVING SEATTLE

THE BIG
PROBLEM
IN LIFE IS NOT
WHAT WE CAN
DO

IT IS KNOWING
WHAT TO DO

AND WHERE
TO START

WHY.

01

"The Weight of Lies," by The Avett Brothers.

The Ride to San Francisco: iTunes is on shuffle and it's the first song. It's sunny, a bit chilly and Mt Rainier is towering over the city. I sit, think, reflect, and ask myself: Why?

δ

Am I really writing a book?

Do I really have something that I want to tell my friends, family, people in my life that I believe can help us all build, live and create better careers? Better lives? I think I do. A year ago I would have never said what I am about to say. I would have never done what I am about to do. This book is a journey, a life, a guide that comes from real stories, real people and real advice that I use myself every day. I am writing this specifically for my best friends and family— my mom, my brother, my dad and my sister. If others find value in it, then that is awesome. This book is geared toward careers and business.

Since most of us work half of our waking lives, our career has more of an impact on our happiness, our success and our future than we believe. My goal isn't to tell you what to do—instead it is to show you a path that you may not have known. As much as this is a book for careers, it is a book for life and my random thoughts on it.

As I leave Seattle on a train to San Francisco, I can't help but smile and think about my life and how fortunate I feel to be where I am today. But at this moment in my life when I feel inspired to create this book I stop and ask myself, "Why?" Why have all of these great moments happened to me? This book will be a reflection of more than twenty years of thoughts that I have saved to create this book.

Here is the catch: I have spent two years saving every single event, topic, method that I have used to get me where I am today. The bigger hook is that I am planning to write this entire book on this one trip, one page at a time, one topic per page, on my way to San Francisco, my journey around San Francisco, and on the train ride back to Seattle.

This book is going to be an adventure, a journey, and no matter what, the minute I pull into Seattle on Monday night that will be the end of this book. That will determine the end. My goal is to write one topic at a time so that anyone can open to any page and read one thing for that day and maybe they can do something, anything, today that will help them get where they want to go.

I feel that the biggest problem in life is not what we can do, it is knowing what to do and where to start. Start small with one thing. There is an overload of information everywhere and if I write this one topic at a time that will be real, raw, and you will experience the trip to San Francisco along with me. I am sure I will get writers block, feel frustrated, and have emotions pouring out of me. But most of all, I will be grateful for this entire trip.

If you are reading this, I thank you and I hope that I can help you. Most of all realize that you can reach out beyond this book and talk to me if you really need anything. I am here and I will do my best to help (but realize that I do not have all of the answers). This book is just my thoughts and stories from a single train ride. Feel free to be a critic and judge as you please. You may have to BS at some point in your life, perception is reality, but when we cut the BS, better things happen. I write this to hopefully make you think and act rather than tell you what you should do.

Here's to writing a book on a four-day trip and train ride to San Francisco. I will try to write this in under 24 hours.

I hope you enjoy the ride.

JUST SAY HI
AND
MAKE
SOMEONE
SMILE

SHANE MAC

RELATIONSHIPS ARE ALL THAT WE HAVE.

02

"Over And Over Again," by Tim McGraw and Nelly.

As my brother drops me off at the train station I think about how much he means to me. I think about my family. I write this. That first part took me twenty minutes which is not good for having so many topics in this notepad that I want to talk about. I need to step up my game.

δ

I sit here alone on the train and think about how complicated life is sometimes. I wonder how it used to be when we didn't have all of this "stuff." I look out the window at buildings, large factories, and everything that we have created in this world and ask myself, "Does this really mean anything?"

Lately I have been focused on the simpler things in life—the "stuff" that really matters. I realize that the only feeling that truly made me smile everyday was when I talked to the people that I care about. My iPhone doesn't make me happy, the voice coming through it does. All these apps, gadgets, buildings—everything for that matter—they don't make me smile and think about how much I love what I do. The people I know do. It is the people and my relationships with them that really matter. Done. Simple as that. All we have in life are relationships, so we better start spending more time building new ones and rebuilding old ones. Build bridges, Rebuild bridges, never Burn Bridges.

Many people build relationships, but then forget about them. It is not enough to build them and hope they stay around forever. It is Work. Time. Love. Passion. A lot of effort to keep a relationship going, working, better over time, but that is life and that is all we have, so right now call, walk next door, or say hello to someone you wouldn't have otherwise. Start right now. Go. With the internet you have the ability to talk to anyone in the world. Anyone. Try telling someone you don't know that you like what they do and ask them how their day is going. Don't walk in the door asking for something for yourself. Ever. Just say Hi and make someone smile.

TAKING NOTES & INDEXING.

03

"Wrapped Up In You," by Garth Brooks.

A stream is off to the right and a few geese lay nesting, awaiting the arrival of springtime.

δ

I am starting to laugh as I write this section of the book because taking notes and indexing them seems like such a dumb topic to talk about, but it has changed my life. Not kidding. No joke. A simple notebook along with the method of taking notes has changed my way of thinking, acting, building, creating, remembering, and most of all, enabling others (which I will get to later).

Damn, something on this train smells like shit. Is that me? Phew.

For starters, I used to steal notes in college. Yeah, I was that guy. I didn't do busy-work stuff. Notes were dumb. I thought this because for the few times I actually took notes I would get to the end of the notebook and throw it away. Done. Gone. Garbage. Yup, just another useless semester of notes. That was the problem. If you can't find what you have created in your notebook then you are right, it is useless.

It all started with a blog post by Tim Ferriss about how he takes notes. When I first read it I didn't really think it would have the effect that it did. Think about how many blogs, books, or other stuff you read or watch every day and think about how you just open another tab, another tab, another tab, another tab, and another tab and by the end of the day you have read so much "stuff" yet you have not remembered any of it that you can actually act on. Sound like you? Shit, sounds like all of us. If we don't take ourselves offline and slow down, think, write, create, we will spend half of our lives just consuming stuff that we will never remember. Start building things that matter and take yourself offline to get things done. Then go online if that is your career.

Here is how it works:

Life is about what we remember but, more importantly, what we act on and create. (This book would not be in progress right now if it weren't for that notebook.) Tim Ferris says, "It is not our ability to take notes, it is our ability to find them later." That's it. That's the secret.

Indexes: so every book has one right? Why don't notes? It is so simple and here is what I learned:

1. Buy a notebook. A larger, hard cover one that will last but is easy to carry around. Now take a minute and number every page 1, 2, 3, etc.
2. Take notes when you read anything—a book, a blog post that is worth remembering, a speech, or any other document.

LIFE IS ABOUT WHAT WE ACT ON AND CREATE

3. Use the notebook to create your own posts, products, designs, business plans, anything ... really, anything.
4. When you finish a page, take a moment and write key points on that page in the bottom right hand corner of the page (or somewhere that is easy to find).
5. Go to the front cover and write what is on that page and place the page number next to it. Don't worry about rewriting another line if you use more than one page for the same book or project as you can just add more page numbers next to that topic.

You are on your way to creating a notebook that will last forever and will have you remembering and creating in no time. If you index an entire book with all of the key points then you can do an entire book review a year from now in under 10 minutes. Before you continue this book, go buy a notebook ... and index it. :)

Once you do it for yourself, go buy all of your friends and family one. Here is a quick story that I did last Christmas:

I was at Barnes & Noble this year and about to buy my family all books for Christmas. I had about $250 worth of books in my hands and when I got to the register I had this moment of "What the F*** am I doing?" I am going to buy my family books when I used to hate getting books and I have no idea if they really want to read them. Stop. Think. Don't do this. I am just buying these to have some tangible thing to give because that is what I am supposed to do. No. Not me. Not today. I took them all back and grabbed about 20 Moleskines (journals) instead. I spent a day and wrote a message to every person in my family. A note, a thank you, a message that I never knew I had to say to so many people in my family. I sit here tearing up at this moment because that one instance was one of the most incredible feelings, gifts, moments that I had ever felt.

I gave a notebook to every person with something I never knew I had to say to each of them. I asked them to create, write, make something that they never thought they could. Now my Grandma, Mom, Dad, and others call me and tell me about the stories, thoughts, ideas, they are writing and that it was the best present they had ever received. A notebook. So simple. Enabling others to do more is my goal in life and a big part of this book. I also was able to give $250 to St. Jude to help children fight cancer. That's a true Christmas and Michelle Roberts, a girl who fought and beat that damn disease, this goes out to you. Love you.

So in the end, take notes and then help others start making and taking notes too by getting them all a notebook ... (and this book).

PEOPLE AND COMPANIES DON'T KILL CAREERS

BOREDOM KILLS CAREERS

WORK IS LIFE.
REALIZE THAT
AND DON'T
SETTLE.

04

Song "Miss Me Baby," by Chris Cagle.

A ship is sitting in the Sound—full of oil maybe? Not sure. It looks so massive, yet calm. I think about our dependence on oil and every ship that has to cross the ocean full of what we see as a need in our life.

Alright so I am onto the third topic and almost an hour into the book. The scenery is getting awesome and more inspiring by the minute. It is starting to set in that I still have 23 hours left of writing. I smile and think about how people think I am a nut case and now I sit here thinking they might be right. Nonetheless, here we go... no more stalling.

δ

Work. Almost every family member, old friend, or person I meet tells me the same thing. "I can't wait till the weekend. I can't wait to get off work. I hate work." Hate? Really? Why? I always ask the same question. When most of us spend more than 15,000 hours a year at work we have to figure out what we hate, why we hate it, and change it. I am not a dreamer who thinks we should all live the dream, but I do think we should like (love) what we do.

I try to answer this question all the time and I look at my life to see what makes me not hate my job. I have a day job. I like my day job. I don't think it is the "day job" most people hate, it is the "job." We spend our lives thinking that we have one path to take, one place to go, one point to reach. I disagree completely. There is too much out there to ever know what you want to do so I think it is about figuring out what you don't want to do. If you don't like it, move on. Check it off the list. Jump.

I hear so many people tell me they hate what they do but they don't know what else is out there. Maybe that is the wrong approach. Does anyone that you work with know that you hate your job? Have you told your boss? One main problem in "corporate" America, IMHO, is that many people feel scared to talk about what they don't like about their job.

Please realize that if no one knows what you are thinking, they cannot help. I know, I know, but they are awesome for just offering me the job so I should just appreciate what I have, right? Yes, always be considerate, but realize that if you are not happy, passionate, and excited about what you are doing you will do it half-assed. That is just life. If you don't like something you will not want to keep doing it. If no one will listen to you then run on. Try your hardest to find another path while you have the steady income at your current job. Don't ever feel bad for leaving a company. That's business. We are people. Be respectful.

We spend too much time thinking there is one job for us when in reality any of us could do many different things. I find my passion in the process of creating and it really doesn't matter what I am actually creating. It's mostly about learning.

I believe people and companies don't kill careers. Boredom kills careers.

STOP CONSUMING START CREATING

START DOING THINGS THAT WILL HELP YOU LATER

STOP BEING A CONSUMPTION WHORE.

05

"I Breathe In, I Breathe Out," by Chris Cagle.

"It is so damn beautiful. This train is incredible. Why don't more people take the train?"

δ

I spent days, weeks, months playing the crack box (Xbox) in college. I spent even more time watching TV, talking to people on Facebook, reading newspapers, magazines, blogs, just consuming. Anything. Everything. I was a true Consumption Whore. We all are, to an extent, and we will consume pretty much anything that is put in front of us.

I never thought of it this way until about a year ago when I moved to Seattle. My brother, Max, wouldn't split the cable bill with me for the TV. I was pissed. That's stupid. He told me, "Try to live without TV for a month." If there is one thing that has changed my life more than anything else it is this one thing: it was selling our HD TV on Craigslist just so it would get out of our house.

The internet can be TV as well, but that is our choice. TV is not. You are thinking to yourself right now, this guy is nuts, he is different than me, I love Desperate Housewives (I do too and it's on Hulu). When all we do is consume, we never feel like we are creating and that feeling is what makes people feel good. Creating life, relationships, products, words in a book, anything. Stop consuming, start creating. When you get done with something that you are creating you will smile and be excited. Exact opposite of how you feel after the Bachelor screws over the woman of his dreams after he whored it up with 30 other women. Really people? Come on.

Alright, so I am dogging on TV but it is really everything. In the past few months I have spent minimal time reading books (one, maybe), a few blog posts, and no TV besides a couple of sports games at the bar. I have spent six months being the happiest I have ever been in my life. Why? I have met more people than ever in my life and created a lot of different "stuff" that is all about building better lives and businesses. We feel like we are going to miss out on something, like we need to watch the news, read the paper, read every single blog post that is in our RSS reader. Wrong. Trust me, you will hear about what you need to hear about. (I still heard of Balloon Boy.)

Everyone wants you to think that you must keep up, so they can make a living by having you as their audience. Why do you think every single news story on CNN is breaking news? It is ridiculous. Plus, it is almost all negative and negativity kills more than anything else.

On the internet I think RSS (inbound information) is death. Yes, I believe you should keep a list of people or sites that you want to remember but when you use RSS, email or other networks you are instantly consuming everything that each person is writing. The truth is, like myself, we don't write awesome stuff every post and you will spend more time trying to clear out your RSS reader and email than you will spending time making something for yourself or reading a blog that can help you in your life. You decide when you want to visit websites and when you get there look for the 'featured post' or 'best of' if you want to find what you should read. Everything on the web is inbound information coming at you which we don't ask for. You have to turn it off, take it off your phone, and only consume it when you can act on it.

Today, eliminate a consumption channel. Try it. Just one at first. I bet you will thank me later. Realize that when you are on Facebook updating your status that you can't take that into an interview and point at it. Start doing things that will help you later. Charity, blogging, video, photos, music. Anything. Now.

RESPECT DEFINES US ALL

RESPECT.

06

"A Rap Medley of Ludacris, Twista, and Usher," by SummerStone, my band in college: wow, I sucked.

It is starting to look like the Midwest. Green trees and pastures of grass and farms. Memories.

δ

Respect.

This one word is my theory on life. It is the one word the trumps them all. Everything. I don't care if I am doing business, hanging out, selling something, or bumping into strangers—it's always about respect. It is the one word that defines all of us.

We have to recognize that if we are not respectable, give respect, every day, every interaction, every moment, then nothing else will ever happen. Whether working in a team, selling a product, or meeting new friends: you will not get anything accomplished without a mutual respect for everyone. Those who disrespect?

Ignore and check them off the list. Move on. Are you respectable? If not, time to think about it.

Do you hate for no reason? Belittle people for no reason? Talk down to people for no reason? Think and treat others like you are better than them? Stop. Don't. Listen. Help. All.

TWITTER AS A MENTOR.

07

Song "Chicken Fried," by Zac Brown Band.

Scenery is the same but Chicken Fried just came on the headphones. Time for a fun ass topic ... You know I like my chicken fried.

Why are there not cup holders on this damn train? Trying to balance my Diet Coke and type this is not easy yet doable. Alright, stop bitching, Shane, and write this. Twitter. O Tweet, Tweet, What? Ha. I love this thing.

δ

Many people use Twitter for many different things. Many claim to be experts. Many claim to know how to use it better than others, forgetting that it is 140 characters being typed in a box. Alright, maybe some know how to get people to click on links more but I would argue that is because they have better relationships with the people clicking rather than the actual links and words that they are posting. Alright enough of the technical, general BS that most people say about Twitter.

Twitter changed my life. It sounds crazy and dumb, I know, but it really did. The ability to talk to anyone in the world, anytime, is incredible. It is what I have wanted my entire life. To meet everyone in the world (not gonna happen) and to realize that we are all in this game called life together trying to figure it out as we go.

It is different from email, facebook and other networks because it is not about who you already know, it is about who CAN you know. That little difference is the secret to it. Anyone can find and follow anyone. Simple as that.

I don't use it like most people. I use it to talk to people, say hi, and build relationships off of Twitter. I believe you can learn more about a person by what they write than what they verbally say to you. When I like what someone says I reach out to them. I have met more people in the last six months who have inspired me to do more, be more, better others, and create things than in the past twenty combined. I never would have thought what has happened to me could have happened because of Twitter. I just landed an amazing job because of a crazy Twitter story.

We just got to a train station. I have no idea where we are. Damn, I have ADDDDDDDDDDDDDDDDDDDDDDDD.

Mainly though, Twitter is my mentor. Not the tool, the voices. Twitter is a message every morning telling me that I can do anything if I put my heart into it and bust my ass. It is a voice that is NOT saying "No, Can't, Don't, What if?" It's that voice saying "Why not, go for it, you can do anything you want." Most importantly, it is saying, "We are here to help and we are all in this together."

With that said, we must realize that every single Twitter, Facebook and other social media experience are completely unique to every single user. You can't call your best friend and say how about the Twitter feed last night? You can if you follow the same people or were in a Twitter chat but for the most part every experience is unique. Just remember that the next time someone hates Twitter or Facebook. Remind them that following 100 idiots that talk about taking a shit is not what you see every day and it's not what Twitter is all about. Twitter's job is to enable communication. Your job is to determine which messages are valuable.

For starters, go to *@shanemac* (me) and look at all of the people that I list if you need some guidance. I create lists for all of them because everyday they inspire me to do more. Be more. This book is a perfect example of that inspiration in action.

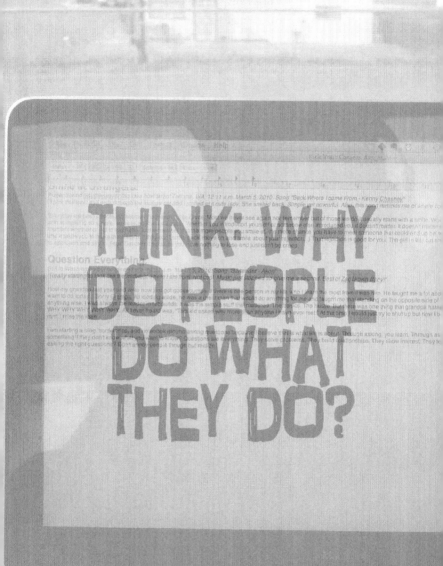

SHANE MAC

LOOK AT THE METHOD, NOT THE MESSAGE.

08

"Shout," by Otis Redding.

"A little bit softer now, A little bit softer now, A little bit softer now, A little bit softer now, HOLY SHIT SHOUT IS ON."

Hey hey hey hey. Shout just came on and the lady across the aisle is probably like why is this guy throwing his arms in the air. (Joke but I am bouncing my head a lot and she is looking at me.) Time out, going to introduce myself... BRB, Deborah. Nice lady.

"I'm Yours," by Jason Maraz just came on and as I see all the land that is out here it makes me think about how busy, crowded, and fast we live in the city and how I forget how much land is out here. This world is so much bigger, physically, than we think.

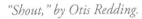

δ

I spend my life thinking about things. Thinking about why people do what they do. Why do I do what I do? Why am I about to buy this product from this sales guy? Why am I buying a sham-wow off this infomercial?

Instead of just listening to the message all the time—Stop. Rewind. Re-do. Think. Rewind. Watch again. Look at the method that got you to do what you are about to do. This is great in both business and life. If you want to start a company, get to the next level in your career, or just start something new find someone who is doing what you want to do successfully and look at all of their methods they use to get things done.

Writers block ... what was I thinking about?

Oh, right: Look at how they go about selling, running, or leading and then recreate what they are doing. We spend way too much time trying to recreate the wheel when we can just use methods that others are using and tailor them to work for us.

Alright, sidetracked, this scenery sucks but Paradise City just came on so I am getting stoked.

Next time you are about to buy, respond, act on something take a minute to reflect on it. Re-watch the commercial, rethink the process, and figure out what it was that got you to do what you are about to do. Then write that down (in the notebook) and use it. This is especially helpful in the online world. Why do people sign up for things? What makes someone do, give, react? It is a fun game to figure out and you will get better at it as you go.

Bathroom Break.

FIND SOMEONE DOING WHAT YOU WANT AND LOOK AT HOW THEY GET THINGS DONE

FEAR

GET OVER IT BECAUSE YOU HAVE NOTHING TO LOSE

SHANE MAC

SMILE AT STRANGERS.

09

"Back Where I come From," by Kenny Chesney.

I pick this topic as I walk through the lounge car and I smile at a cute lady. She smiles back. Simple yet powerful. Also, this song reminds me of where I come from and all those people who I love and miss in the Midwest.

Every day we pass people, sometimes thousands, in our lives. Most we never see again, nor remember, but of those we do it usually starts with a smile. When life is all about relationships stop and think about how many of them started with something so simple, so easy, so true as a smile.

Whether you introduced yourself or someone else introduced you it doesn't matter. It doesn't matter if it is a guy or a gal. It is just about a smile and then you will know with that moment whether or not to say hello. Just remember that the more people you smile at, the more chance you have to meet someone that could end up being a lifelong friend.

Be the enabler and start smiling. Many times it takes you to make them smile.

Most people don't do this and it takes *you* to make them smile. If they don't smile back, move on and smile about your rejection.

That rejection is good for you. The girl in this car smiled back and I might have to take a lunch break for ten minutes ... Oh the nerves to approach and say hi.

Fear.

Get over it because you have nothing to lose.

REJECTION IS GOOD FOR YOU

ASK
WHY

QUESTION EVERYTHING.

10

"Bartender," by Akon.

Really starting to look like the Midwest where I am from. Not cool. Music just stopped so give me a second. Best of Zac Brown Baby!

δ

I lost my Grandpa last year and right now just got goose bumps. If there is one person in my life who I learned the most from, it was him. He taught me a lot about people in general, and I learned from his "methods" some things that I do not want to do today— sorry, Gramps. All kidding aside, he was a great man who would do anything for me, and taught me that standing on the opposite side of the basketball hoop when a player shoots will get you more rebounds than anything else. I was always the leader in rebounds. It was the simple stuff that mattered. The basics. The hustle. But there was one thing that Grandpa hated. I asked "why?" more than any damn kid in the world. Always.

Why WHY WHY WHY WHY WHY WHY. All I ever

heard was, "This kid asks 'why' more than anyone I have ever met." At the time I would just try to shut up but now I believe that single question has turned me into who I am today.

Sorry for that rant, I miss the man.

I am starting a blog, conference and notebook around asking questions, because I believe that is what life is about. Through asking, you learn. Through asking, you let others know what you want to know. How could someone tell you something if they don't know what you want to know? Questions are everything. They solve problems. They build relationships. They show interest. They tell stories about people. Through questions we, together, find answers. Are you asking the right questions? Don't annoy people, though, and realize that no one, including yourself, has all of the answers—so don't kid yourself. Start asking.

If you want to find people and connect with them online, then head out to every social network you know of and find people who have questions. You will find more people than you ever imagined that have questions and you have the answer to them. Those simple answers will build relationships that can help you out in the future.

ASK QUESTIONS

THIS IS WHAT
LIFE IS ABOUT

SET DEADLINES

SHANE MAC

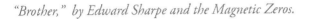

GET SHIT DONE.

11

"Brother," by Edward Sharpe and the Magnetic Zeros.

This river looks like someone took a shit in it for 30 years. Disgusting and reminds me of the Illinois River I grew up in.

δ

You know exactly what I am talking about with this section. You wait until the last minute and you always seem to get it done. Somehow, someway. It is Parkinsin's Law. *(I had to go grab my notebook that had the quotes in it)*. It states that, "The demand of a resource tends to expand to match the supply of resource." All it is saying is that you will get the work done in the time allowed. If you give yourself two weeks then it will take you two weeks because you know you have that much time. If you have three days you will get it done in three days.

With that said, I understand that there are limitations. Some things have long timelines, but the point is to set harder deadlines and force yourself to focus on each element or task with a tight deadline. If you focus on eliminating the time available you will find yourself getting more done, quicker, and (I find) with better results. Start setting tighter deadlines and start getting more things done.

LEARN.
LEARN.
LEARN.

12

"F*** the Popo," by Corey Smith.

I am getting thirsty and hungry so after this I am going to run downstairs for some food. Nothing out the window worth talking about besides BNSF train cars and graffiti.

δ

If there is one thing that you can never stop doing in life it is Learning. We can never know enough and never know it all. We have to learn from each other and realize that we all have something that we can teach others. I believe this is a big problem in corporations today with the hierarchy's of job positions that exist. People at the top think they have all the answers and they have nothing to learn from the folks below them. That is crap.

We all need to keep learning everyday 'til the day we die. You can learn by creating, trying, reading, talking, anything. Just try to learn something new every day. We need to realize that life is changing so fast nowadays that no one really knows what is right and what is wrong. I say it all the time but I believe that age is silenced by one's passions, ambition, and our ability to learn from those who are willing to teach.

Go on Google and search for something you want to know about, ask a professor, something, or just start writing or creating something you like and start doing this daily. You will be surprised how far you will be in no time.

WE CAN NEVER KNOW ENOUGH

LEARN

ANYTHING CAN BE A CAREER

IF SOMEONE ELSE WANTS WHAT YOU HAVE TO OFFER

DON'T LISTEN TO YOUR PARENTS ALL THE TIME.

13

"Oh Happy Day," by Sister Act 2.

Ya, Sister Act 2 is my favorite movie.

δ

I love Sister Act 2. The message is simple: Follow your dreams. When you show your Mom (or anyone) that your dream can come true, they will be proud of you. The point is that the mother in the movie thought she was right, thought she knew what Lauren Hill had to do and told her what she couldn't do. Lauren didn't listen. She followed her dream and her mother was proud. The truth is that while parents are great (I have the best) and they only want to help us, they can sub-consciously kill our dreams by the fear of the unknown. It is not their fault that they don't see what I see, it is just what they know. They have spent 40 years working for retirement and doing what they were expected to do. That is not wrong.

I am not saying to do something completely crazy but if you totally believe in something then you have to fight the "don't," "no," "that's not a career," talk. Remember that anything can be a career as long as someone else wants what you have to offer. It is that simple and if you believe in it enough then go for it. When you make it they will be there fist pumping with you and if you don't make it, guess what, they will still be there to catch you most of the time. Even though they are awesome and want to help it is those simple comments that can stop you from just giving something a try.

That is what this life is about. Trying new things and finding out what you want to do. If you don't like it then check it off the list but remember that you will never know unless you try. What do you want to do in your life? Right now? What have you said in the past year, "I would love to do that."

Do it. Now.

TRY NEW
THINGS

AND FIND
OUT WHAT YOU
WANT
TO DO

BE HONEST ABOUT WHAT YOU DON'T KNOW

I AM ALWAYS RIGHT = YOU ARE AN IDIOT.

14

"Black Betty," by ZZ Top.

Really getting tired of this scenery... Still haven't eaten lunch. Can't stop.

δ

"I kissed a girl and I liked it" just came on. I totally used to pump my fist to this song in my hometown bar in Bartonville, Illinois. Anyways, I used to hang out with a lot of people at that small town bar that thought they were always "right." They thought they had life figured out and they had all the answers. Don't be that person. Enough Said.

Truth is, we don't really know much. I've received more jobs, raises, etc., by being honest about what I didn't know rather than what I did know. Don't try to bullshit the system. Show your willingness to learn rather than your arrogance to know it all.

</Rant over.>

(That's for you code geeks.)

LIVE OUTSIDE OF YOUR JOB

SHANE MAC

CORPORATE LADDER IS BS.

15

"Free Falling," by John Mayer.

Starting to get in the flow... A guy just sat down next to me who was sitting by the girl across the train car who I smiled at. Maybe he got scared?

δ

The ladder is an image that is created, and more times than not makes people feel like they are not getting anywhere because they are not climbing up it. It is about realigning our expectations, realizing that the ladder is actually just a false belief that there is a top. Realize that the ladder only leads to the base of another ladder. Should you strive to climb it? Always strive to do more, but just change how you see it.

Here is how I did it and somehow found a voice with Executives.

1. Live outside your job title. It is so easy to always focus on the task at hand. Sure, you need to get it done, but how can you

help other departments? We are all new to this game of life and work and we can all benefit from each other.

2. Say Hi. It is so easy to forget that if people don't know you, know what you do, and like you, then how can they promote you? Every day, walk by a person who you can benefit from knowing and can help you get to the next step and just say hi. You will be surprised how far that goes...

I hope the ladder dies and we start working together and realizing that we can all learn from each other. That is the new model of business. That is the new model of life. We spend half of our waking life working, remember that and start building relationships at work.

IT IS NOT WHO YOU KNOW...

16

"Life in a Northern Town," by Sugarland.

I am getting distracted and mind is spinning. Scenery is getting better and the sun is still shining really bright.

δ

How many times have you heard this: "It is all about who you know." There is some truth to that, but I would beg to differ because the statement reads in past tense. I believe it is all about who CAN you know and HOW you know them. My friend Matt Sage added the second part about HOW and I totally agree. When we now have the ability to pretty much talk to anyone in the world through our communication channels it is all about connecting with people who will better us and then building a relationship with them beyond twitter, facebook, email, etc. It is how you know people nowadays because when we have thousands upon thousands of connections the quality of the relationship is more important than the number of followers, fans, or whatever the hell else you have in your crackberry (mobile device for those of you who don't know what that means).

After I listened to a speech by Tim Ferris about a challenge he gave to college students—where they had to try and contact the most unreachable person they could through some of Tim's methods—I realized, without even noticing it, I had been doing this my entire life.

The first step is getting over the fear. We are all the same in life but some of us do more than others and may have different limitations but for the most part we are all the same.

The second step is to never walk in the front door asking for something. (You can ask them how they feel about an intellectual question but never ask for something for yourself.) You should acknowledge their work, their word, or just let them know that you are thankful for what they have done. If you hear no response then what did you have to lose, an email? Try it today. Pick five people or companies that you want to contact and send them an email just to let them know who you are (quick bio that says you are in college or in a career and that you value what they do) and then ask them a question that is not about the job, career, or what they usually hear or just tell them thanks. You want to get a response that is an answer to a question or a thank you. You can feed off that when you get it and build from there.

You can stop there, keep trying to contact them, or you can get creative. If you are on the internet you can usually see who the person is connected too. Here is what I would do:

I would look at who that person talks to and connect with them in the same manner as I stated above and try to build

THE FIRST STEP IS GETTING OVER THE FEAR

LIVE OUTSIDE
YOUR JOB
TITLE

relationships with them. Build relationships with people before you ever need to ask for anything. This is for careers as much as life. Build relationships first and then ask for the job or ask for the introduction in this case later. The biggest point here though is that you better have something worth getting introduced for. Think about what you want out of that connection. Have something to say when you walk in the door. Don't just sit there and think someone should talk to you because you are yourself. Do something worth talking about and actually know and care about the person you are connecting too. Don't just do it for the sake of connecting.

Some people tell me they don't want to know anyone else—and that is fine, but not me—I believe in this Stowe Boyd quote: "I am made better by the sum of my connections and so are my connections." You can say you don't want to meet anyone else in your life but then when you need a job, a hand, or just a friend to talk to—I bet your opinion will change.

Main point to remember: Have something to say when you walk through the door. Be interesting, have a story, have a purpose and most of all don't be scared. I have a lot of case studies on how to approach people on twitter, email, and real life as well. You can email *casestudy@shanemac.me* if you want to check them out! (It is pretty amazing the people you can connect to.)

1:37 PM

5:40 PM

OREGON

FOR DECISIONS, REALIZE THAT THERE IS NO RIGHT AND WRONG

YOU WILL LEARN AS YOU GO

WILL YOU MARRY ME? NO, WTF! RELATIONSHIP THOUGHTS.

17

"I Run," by Lady Antebellum.

I have never been to Portland and we can get off the train to get food and a beer so I think I might. This book could get interesting after a brewski. Then I can write my thought on relationships.

Time now is actually 2:19 p.m. and they didn't have any booze. Damn. That took forever. I have written one Topic in the past hour. Back on it even though I just had the plainest turkey sandwich in history. Leaving Portland now and back to my seat. Seat 1 in car 1113 on the Coastliner Express.

δ

A lot of my friends are getting married, some of my friends have already gotten married, but one of my friends asked his girlfriend to marry him and she said NO. I thought about that for a second and I wanted to share my thoughts on this. In my own life I would know the answer before I ever asked. Call me a sissy but if I am REALLY going to spend the rest of my life with someone I really want them to say Yes out of a surprise and then feel obligated to hold that promise that was made in an instant moment of surprise. I love the unexpected, but I feel like I have seen some of my friends' relationships and marriages end and they all say that they didn't feel it before the wedding but felt like they didn't know how to turn back.

Here is another thought: If that happens... RUN!

Here is a letter I wrote to a friend asking me for relationship advice, *(which is pretty funny to me in the first place.. and Britney Spears just came on... It's Britney, Bitch.)*

"As for decisions, realize that there is not right and wrong and you will learn as you go. Stop seeing things as failures and realize it is about the process of making things work or finding that they don't work that life is all about. That is the same for business. Stop shooting for dreams and start adjusting as you go... Realigning your expectations is a huge shift in how you view life and will help you be a lot happier with every decision you make and how that only leads to new decisions. Let them happen, react, adjust, and realize that in life all we have are relationships so stop trying to figure it out and just work on them. We can't figure that shit out. None of us. Ever. There is no right or wrong answer to it. Just recognize what doesn't work, do less of it and find what does work and do more of it. Be open to change.

I hope you do what is best for you and strive to stay positive and happy in all you do. All I would say is, every day, do you feel like you are better because of the person you are with? If you can't answer that then you have found your answer. If you ever need anything let me know..."

PROSTITUTES CAN TEACH US BUSINESS AND CAREER TIPS.

18

"Watching Airplanes," by Gary Allan.

δ

Prostitution is the oldest known business in the world. We can learn something from that.

You know where to find them.

You know who they are.

You know what they offer.

You know how much they cost and that you will have to pay more to get more.

Make sure you follow all four of those closely and get your ass on the corner so people can find you, like you, test you, and get more out of you. Do people know where to find you? Do recruiters know where they can get a quickie? Be a hooker. *(It's a joke for all of you stiffs out there.)*

I BELIEVE THAT WE WILL NEVER KNOW EXACTLY WHAT WE WANT TO DO

TRUE LEADERS BRING OUT THE TRUTH, THE NEGATIVE, AND ADDRESS.

19

"What I Got (acoustic)," by Sublime.

It is starting to flow again about like this song... Lovin... is what I got baby...

δ

I have never really considered myself a leader. I just always try to help out where I can and help others see that they can do what they didn't think they could. A lot of people can do that. What I have really found is that it is more about letting people know it is alright to talk about the bad, the negative, the things they don't like. If you can't get people to open up about what is not working, then they will just keep digging a bigger hole and become more unhappy.

Here is what I mean: I will use a phone call with a friend the other day as an example. This happens often to me.

Me: Hey man, how is life and your job?

Friend: It's going good man. (With no enthusiasm.)

Me: Awesome, what are you doing at work...

(This will go on for an extended time... and then the conversation usually ends like this:)

Friend: Man, actually, I hate my job. I just don't know where to look or what I want to do.

Me: You never will. I believe that we will never know exactly what we want to do. You have to start building better relationships *(see other tips in this book)* and find a job that you think you would enjoy and that could be a challenge.

It is about working at a company or starting a company where you feel passionate about the product you are producing. You have to have a sense of pride in the end product or you will never excel to what you can truly be. Find your flaws, talk about what you don't like, amplify them, be honest about them, and try to get others to do the same.

I think that is a leadership quality that is often forgotten.

Am I a leader? I don't know exactly. I know that I love being part of a team and helping others get to their full potential. I find more reward in enabling others than what I do myself sometimes. Leaders don't need a title and can come from any levels. If you want to be seen as a leader, you will have to be one before you are seen as one. Start today by giving some fist pumps around the office and saying "Let's do something awesome." It's a start and it can grow from there. Give everyone a purpose.

JOB TITLES CAN HURT MORE THAN THEY HELP.

20

"Tonight," on Rent, The musical.

I have a lot crazy variety of music on my computer and listening to Rent makes me wanna dance.

δ

It has been about five hours into this ride. I quit my job yesterday and this is my first day without a job title. I was a project manager. I do not like project management. It is not hard to do and is more like Professional Organizer than anything. I did a lot more than that at my job—but it was that title, the pay grade, that level, that expectation that hurts companies and the people that need to work together.

Don't get me wrong, I think we need to be clear on the role of individuals, but I feel like the way job titles are implemented in larger organizations makes the top feel entitled and the bottom feel used. I never felt that way at all and I was able to be on many different teams and learn from many different people but I didn't see that happening much besides myself.

Job titles muffle innovation in some cases, and I hate when people think they are better than someone else. I hate when people feel like they need to work hard to get the job done in front of you so you can get to the next job title. Why is it always about moving up and not just working collaboratively?

So do I think it is the title that is bad? No. Not at all. I think the fact that people put all of their coolness, arrogance, and value on a single title is the problem and people need to get over themselves and help others do better work. Most of the time it is not in the top leadership's best interests to make you better because you would take their job if you moved up... The irony of the ladder is that someone has to fall if you climb to the top unless the company has growth. Most of the time I think someone falls, though.

JOB TITLES CAN MUFFLE INNOVATION

THE TRUTH IS MOST PEOPLE DON'T OWN ANYTHING

WORTH MORE THAN 10,000 DOLLARS

4 WHEELS AND $40,000 IN DEBT. BUT YOU ARE COOL. HA, NOT.

21

"Back at One," by Brian McKnight.

δ

This is a message to all of my friends back at home who love to look cool. I love you.

I used to have a Mustang. I used to think I was so damn cool in it. (It was slick.)

Speaking of that, I am going through a town right now that looks like my hometown and the Tootsie Roll just came in the headphones. Oooooo shit. Alright, back to the topic...

I got over that really quick and realized the only chicks I was thinking I could pick up (idiot by the way) with the car were the same ones who valued different things than me in life. The truth is, most people don't own anything over $10,000. This isn't about cars. It is about flaunting what you have or buying stuff for the sake of image and perception. I used to do it. I thought it was cool. It is fake.

Buy things that you want. If you enjoy something then buy it but stop buying, flaunting, showing off stuff to fulfill your own ego. Whether it is cars, money, boats or anything for that matter. Do it for self fulfilling enjoyment and happiness, not for some bullshit perception.

I am spending way too much time trying to pick good songs... I just picked "Back Where I come from again," ... Next topic... Need to get inspired again so about to take some pictures out the window...

HAPPINESS AND SUCCESS ARE CONTAGIOUS.

22

"Back Where I Come From," by Kenny Chesney.

I am in some suburban neighborhoods and very uninspiring. Hopefully I will get into Northern California soon because I hear that is amazing.

δ

A year and two months ago I moved to Seattle. I left a relationship, family, friends, and a lifetime behind. Hard. It was hard. But it was exciting and the fact that I had my brother waiting for me in Seattle along with a great job that was doubling my salary made it a lot easier. (Doubled salary is relative to where you live: remember that.) My house in Seattle that we rent would cost $425,000 to buy, while in Illinois it might cost $100,000. Anyways, I moved. I started working. I worked hard and met some people while getting my new life started. I spent seven months figuring the corporate life out. Figuring out what to do with my new-found freedom. Then it happened.

I met the right person, persons, people. The right people. It all happened so fast over the last six months. One person who believed in me and extended their hand to help me get off my feet and start believing in what I was doing was all it took. I met more great people, and more great people, and pretty soon I had some folks looking up to me. Some people asking me for advice. Really? Me? I heard a quote once that "You are the average of your five friends," and I could not agree more. Don't get me wrong, I still love all of my friends I have met through my entire life and I hope we can do good together.

If you feel down, upset, or you feel like you can't find your true path then work to find people who inspire you, better you, and contact them. Try to cross paths with them and do it in a 'normal' way. Set yourself up to be at the same place they are and start building a relationship in that manner. Set out to find people in new ways. Use twitter, email, facebook, linked in, whatever. Don't be creepy about it, though, and start surrounding yourself with people who inspire you. Sounds cliché but it is true. You will find yourself in a better place.

STOP SENDING ME QUOTES YOU DON'T ACTUALLY DO.

23

"Shame," by The Avett Brothers.

The picture outside would suck so I just took a picture of some quotes in Evernote. "Be the change you want to see in others." - Ghandi.

δ

Dad. This. Is. For. You. My Dad is amazing. He really is. Here is the problem, though. Every morning I get a quote of the day from him that are usually great quotes that I cling onto like a hawk, but then I stop and think about it. I think. Stop and think about the email or phone calls that I used to get at nighttime. His true word contradicted the quotes he was sending. Biggest example was the old "Live your dream but be realistic." This was not a problem and was not unexpected. (I had a lil talk with Dad and now he is all about being a teammate.)

I see this all the time in life, though. So many people talk. Share. Spread great words of wisdom, yet never practice what they are preaching. That drives me nuts and I really would love everyone to act on what inspires them and hopefully this book will help you do that. You really can do anything you want as long as you have drive, passion, and focus over time. Next time you send a quote, stop, think, and make sure you are actually sending something that you actually do.

SHORTCUTS DON'T WORK.

24

"I and Love and You," by The Avett Brothers.

*I think this is where witchcraft happens or some shit? Who knows...
I hope there aren't any witches on this train. I beat her ass with the
broomstick next to me.*

δ

This will be quick. People spend so much time trying to try
the next big thing. Reading about the next shortcut or secret to
business, losing weight, or careers. The secret to all of these topics.
Keep wasting your time. In the past six months here is what I have
done and how.

Landed an awesome new job at a startup. Lost 25 pounds. Started
some companies.

How? I don't fall for the bullshit and I make stuff simple. Here is
what I did, for each one above.

I tweeted a girl about coffee. We met. Through her, I met the founder of the company at a pool hall. I built a relationship. I then saw a job opening. I asked him to join me in projects I was doing outside of my job. I thought I had a passion and skill that could help. I signed the papers yesterday and I start next week. Done. Took four months. Patience.

I ate three things a day. Not three meals with five sides. Three things. Example: one bowl of cereal, one big sandwich, and one salmon for dinner. As much as people make this complicated it is not. 1 calorie = heat. Stay under a certain number by eliminating all of the sides and crap. Screw points, counting calories, etc, as that is even confusing as hell. Just count to three. One main entree per meal. Only weigh once a week. Every day is too much and you will ride an emotional train because of fluctuations of weight.

I had something that someone else wanted. That is a business. Seem simple? It is. People make it seem so hard but if you have something that someone else wants and will pay for then you have a business.

IF YOU HAVE
SOMETHING
THAT
SOMEONE
ELSE WANTS AND
WILL PAY FOR

THEN YOU
HAVE A
BUSINESS

EVERY
BUSINESS
STARTS WITH
ONE PRODUCT
ONE IDEA
AND A FIRST
CUSTOMER

START A LEMONADE STAND—I MEAN A BUSINESS.

25

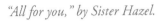

"All for you," by Sister Hazel.

I love one-hit wonders.

δ

Whether you are getting a job, want to be an entrepreneur, or be a business owner, the lesson is the same. If you are starting a job and need some skills to talk about, then running a business is probably one of the best qualities that you can have. You wear a lot of hats and learn how it works. You learn as you go, and with tools such as outright.com, freshbooks.com, and just good old Google you can find about everything that you need to know.

If you want to start a business, I just want you to remember that it doesn't have to be the next biggest thing in the world. It can be something so small, so niche (a lemonade stand), that a lot of people would want. Every business starts with one product, one idea, and a first customer, so remember that. You probably laugh about a lemonade stand but did you forget about coffee? I bet people just like you were laughing 40 years ago when Starbucks was just getting started. If you want to make the next big thing, my advice would be to find some good partners.

For the specific details on starting your business I suggest you pick up Beth Andrus' book "The Essential Business Handbook." It has everything you need.

GENIUS IS 99% PERSPIRATION, 1% INSPIRATION.

26

"All Right Now," by Bad Company.

Green Grass is a growing. Oregon is pretty boring on this train route. All good though. I have a new guy sitting next to me who is snoring like a wolf. Awesomeness. Headphones = Louder. I need another drink so I'm heading to the diner car, then I will chill in the lounge. This guy is on my shoulder practically. Couldn't I at least get a lady friend that wanted my shoulder? Damn. BRB.

Back. That was an adventure. I hate it when people who have no reason to be control freaks yell at people and start abusing the badge on their shirt. Come on, Amtrak employee, really, is this kid going to hurt the steel carts in the diner car? Ridiculous what I just saw. Whatever, moving on. Back to the lounge and looking out the left side of the train.

δ

"Genius is 99% Perspiration, 1% Inspiration." - Thomas Edison. This quote is how I live my life. It isn't about having ideas, it is about acting on them. It is what the company Behance tries to solve every day. People always talk about what they want to do but hardly ever act to accomplish the goal. Why? Because it is hard-ass work. The first part of the quote, "perspiration," says it all. It is a 99:1 ratio. You have to bust your ass for a long time to make something work. I always say the secret is Focus over Time. It is also the ability to recognize a dead idea and filter out the ideas that you don't believe in and probably won't work. I spend most of my time filtering out the bad ideas to find one good idea. Then if I already have a few ideas moving ahead I try to limit taking on any new things until I finish those. (Recently, this is getting pushed to the limits a bit but I have filtered out quite a few things.)

The biggest thing I do in my life though is build things to point at. I used to own a Web Development company. It was a service model. Yeah, we shut that down. Just wasn't me and the only way to grow was to hire more and find more clients. It wasn't our own product and that bothered me.

So nowadays, I build things to point at. I have great teammates running with me who believe in what we are doing and that is all that matters. Once they launch we will adjust, improve, and build more things that last forever. We are in no hurry and want to do things right. That's my new way of life and business. Simple, efficient, and build things that I will be the first person in line to sign up.

make the next big thing, my advice would be to find some good partners.

"Genius is 99% Perspiration, 1% Inspira

South of Salem, Oregon. 3:58 p.m. March 5, 2010. Song "All Right Now - Bad Company"
(I love one hit wonders. Wonder if i'll always be with you.)

"Genius is 99% Perspiration, 1% Inspiration." - Thomas Edison

BUILD THINGS TO POINT AT

"THAT IS DUMB"

YOU ARE DUMB

DUMB IS DEATH
AND THAT
IS DUMB.

27

"Eye of the Tiger," Rocky Soundtrack.

I just bought 2 Jim Beam's and Diet Coke's. Hope I don't start slurring my words. OOOOOOOOOOO SHIT, Eye of the Tiger. ** Head Bobs and an observation. People on this train are looking at me weird. I think they are weird too.**

δ

"That is Dumb."

If I had a dollar for every time someone has said something like that to me in my life, I would be rich. Really rich. The problem is that I understand a lot of people are not like me and they won't get over the dumb and will just not try it because they think they will be dumb.

Here is a true story.

I was a Junior in High School. I have played baseball my entire life. Played hard. Hard as I could. My entire life was around this sport. Summers, friends, everything. The year before I had the best batting average on the team. 107 at bats, only 7 strikeouts. .387 average and the coach's motto was "If you hit, you'll play." Not me. Not this year. I got cut. That was it. Baseball. Life. Friends. It was over. 12 years of trying slashed by one coach's decision and a cold shoulder.

All I say is thank you. Whenever someone hates, says you are dumb, or just is rude ... just say thanks. Thank you. Thank you very much. I am trying out for choir. I was in the lunch line and the choir teacher was behind me and she heard my loud ass singing and said I should try out for choir. Ha, me? Ya right. I was too cool for that.

I told my friends and they said "That's dumb." They said, "You are gay." I laughed and said, yup. Thank you. I joined choir.

Now, today, my friends, family, and every critic I ever had sings my praises and wants to come to a show when I just got awarded best Wedding Band in Seattle, WA. I landed a sponsorship by Miller Lite and played promotional events all through college for them. Yeah, it was and still is awesome but it took me getting over that DUMB moment to get where I am today and I hope the next time you get in that situation you will stop for a second and just do it, say thank you, and step outside of your comfort zone. It is huge.

I find that making fun of yourself makes it easier to do what others call dumb and can give you the confidence and the carefreeness that is needed to just do it. What have you been putting off lately because people might think you are dumb? Do it now and remember: people belittle out of jealousy.

Just smile and say thanks.

STEP
OUTSIDE
OF YOUR
COMFORT
ZONE

WHERE ARE THE PEOPLE SAYING

HELL YEAH!

FEAR.

28

"Goodbye Earl," by The Dixie Chicks.

I haven't even taken a drink of whiskey yet and that took me about 30 minutes to write. Shit. Hold on I am taking a drink. But guess what, "Earl's Gotta Die."

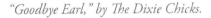

δ

Seth Godin would say it is the "lizard brain." Others would say it is fear of the unknown. I would say it is a lot of factors, but mostly just fear. Fear is invoked by the lizard, as well as your friends, as well as the unknown. The worst part is that most of the time it is invoked subconsciously without anyone even realizing they are causing it.

I think about my situation. How I have had to fight those who would always remind me of what I can't, shouldn't, won't, do. No. No. No. No. No. Where are the people saying "Hell yeah!"? Where are the people who are just honest and say that it is NOT A GOOD IDEA?

Usually people don't tell me why, how, or what I should do they just say something along the lines of, "Hmmm." Subconsciously smashing the dream or idea that I thought would be great.

Twitter. That's what twitter was to me. It was the confidence to say hell yeah, let's do this. It was the power to overcome the failures, because you can see so many other people who are doing great things. Who are willing to help. Everywhere.

Fear is usually created for false reasons. Ask yourself, "If I would do this today what would the consequences be?" Will you die? What will you have to adjust? Life is not about what we can or can't do but rather what we are willing to adjust to allow us to do what we want to do. What do you have to lose? Try something small at first that you would never do and go from there. Once you start getting over the fear it will be helpful in other areas of life.

I am scared shitless to skydive but fearless when it comes to talking to people of any level. Find your strengths, embrace them, and then find your fear and conquer it.

Looks like I am going sky diving.

This Jim Beam tastes awesome.

FAKE.
SUITS, TIES
AND LIES.

29

"We Built this City," by Starship.

I have so many suits that I was going to need to wear everyday when I started working. Ha, what a joke. The 80's tunes rock.

The diner car is open. Screw that. I bet it tastes like cardboard and I like my whiskey diet better, anyways. I just had to send a text message but I turned my phone back off...

δ

I think that this is my favorite topic. I spent my college days thinking that life was about suits and ties. It was about painting pictures and pretending that I was perfect. It was about knowing everything. Being a leader. Fake. Really fake.

I just took a little break to grab some dinner and call Mr. Brett Byrd for some inspiration. Mission Accomplished. Back at it and ONE WHISKEY DOWN.

I believe this is the main problem with business and careers as we know them today: people act differently at work than who they actually are outside of work. Why is that the norm? You want to know why corporations are scared shitless of Social Media...? That is the reason. Everything they have been painting... Sales pitches, marketing plans, and what people do outside of work, are all out there in the open and it is scaring the living crap out of them.

It is crazy to me that people judge and act different at work than they do in other aspects of their life. Yeah, don't show up drunk to a presentation but why does it matter if I got wasted on Saturday night? The judging, the suits, the ties, the lies have got to go if we want to really start building better business, better careers, better lives for everyone.

Side note: I like wearing suits and I think it is totally cool to look good and take that as a metaphor for fake. Thanks.

"MEETINGS USUALLY REPLACE MASTURBATION."

30

"I Still Miss You," by Keith Anderson.

Dinner in a box is gone and a beautiful lake just appeared. The sun is setting and darkness is coming. Been an awesome day though. I think of my first day off work, first day disconnected from most of the world, and smile. laugh. look around. and wonder. wonder if anyone else on this train is writing a book. Is this a book? Shit I don't know. It feels like I type just like this all the time. I will never consider myself an Author.

Can't Touch This just came on... WHAAAAAAAAAAAAAAAAAAAAAA AAAAAAAAAAAAAT!

δ

PLEASE STOP HAVING A MEETING TO GO OVER THE TIMELINE AND STOKING YOUR EGO BECAUSE YOU CAN RUN THE MEETING.

AAAAAAAAAAAAAAAAAAAAAAAAAAAAAAAAAAAHH! AAAAAAA

AAAAAAAAAAAAAAAAAAAAAAAAAHH! AAAAAAAAAAAAAA
AAAAAAAAAAAAAAAAAHH! AAAAAAAAAAAAAAAAAAAAAA
AAAAAAAAAHH! AAAAAAAAAAAAAAAAAAAAAAAAAAAAAA
AAAAHH! AAAAAAAAAAAAAAAAAAAAAAAAAAAAAAAAAHH!
AAAAAAAAAAAAAAAAAAAAAAAAAAAAAAAAHH!

My friend Andrew Swenson wrote something on this topic and said use technology tools and online collaboration methods to go over timelines and the task list. Use meetings for brainstorming, collaboration, and creative scrums. If you are scheduling the meeting then make sure you look organized and have actions that people will do when they leave the meeting.

Here is what I do.

1. Send out an outline with Topics, People, Timelines.
2. Use *http://www.nextup.info/* to insert the outline in and set time for each to-do.
3. Keep everyone on time. People will talk for the amount of time you give them so make it shorter than you would think.
4. Action. Action. Action. Everyone always says it but it is so true. Have something to do out of the meeting.
5. Have someone else take notes.
6. Never have a meeting over 30 minutes.
7. Excuse those who are not needed.

In no time people will see you as a leader just by running the meeting a little differently. You will also save the company money because time is money when we talk about employee's salaries.

THE BS HAS GOT TO GO

IF WE WANT TO BUILD BETTER BUSINESSES CAREERS AND LIVES FOR EVERYONE

Friday, March 5, 2010

5:53 PM

8:56 PM

PROBABLY IN
CALIFORNIA

WE DON'T
REALIZE HOW
MUCH TIME
WE WASTE
ON EMAIL

MOST OF
THOSE EMAILS
DON'T
CREATE
ANYTHING

SHANE MAC

LIMIT EMAIL.

31

"Don't Stop Believing," by Journey.

Just a small town girl. Taking another sip of whiskey... I think I might grab 2 more... Decisions? This train is so peaceful it is incredible. I am just thinking if they would have had a rail bill pass congress like they had the interstate system how awesome that would be because I hate flying. Scares the ssssssshit out of me yet I do it quite often.

δ

Email. Nowadays email is like crack. It never ends and people just send, reply all, reply for the sake of replying, etc. It will kill you. At my old job I probably received 70% of emails that were complete BS in my first 6 months of working there. It was when I addressed it that people started listening.

If I ever forwarded an email I would reply all and ask if there was a better way to get it to the person I forwarded it to. I would ask politely yet make it aware that this didn't make sense. I took myself off of all alias lists that were group lists. If I needed to know, someone would tell me.

It worked great. People started talking more and collaboration started happening outside of email. People started realizing the time drain. People started realizing that their job was pretty much forwarding emails which is why a lot of people probably don't want to make it more efficient.

On another note, I couldn't get by with eliminating email during the day at work but I did take my personal accounts off of my phone and only open them at 5 p.m. every day. It saved me so much time not having to get that red dot off my iPhone all day or having my computer constantly pinging me. We don't realize how much time we waste on email and when we do it is pretty sick to realize that none of those emails are actually creating anything.

One sec, my mom just texted me. Alright, I'm back. She was just checking in on me...

A great way to easily see where all of your time is being spent online is to download *http://www.rescuetime.com* and install on your computer. You don't have to do anything and it will tell you exactly where you are spending all of your time. It's simple and awesome reminder to get stuff done. You can also limit certain sites during the day between certain times.

STOP FORWARDING EMAILS.

BE WHO YOU WANT TO BE THE DAY YOU WALK IN THE DOOR.

32

"Swan Dive," by Sister Hazel.

I really really really still have no idea where I am. Some awesome mountains.

As the sun sets I think about my job I left, the day I have had, and the people I am about to meet for the first time. Jun Loayza and Jenny Blake. Regardless, I am smiling, jamming, and looking around at a lot of other people probably on their way to meet family, friends, anyone. This is the hardest/awesomest trip I have ever taken not talking to anyone the entire time. Talking to myself really.

δ

This comes from a personal experience. I get a job as a project manager and I am seen as a project manager. While I am a project manager I start my own Web Development company and I am seen as a "Founder." As dumb as it sounds, perception matters. People in my company (although not after a few months of busting down walls and proving myself) saw me as a Project Manager while

HAVE
SOMETHING
WORTH
TELLING

people all over the country saw me as a Founder of a company.

I was treated differently. Very differently. Is that how it should be? No, but that is reality and perception plays a large role in who we get to talk too and how we are treated. Sucks. Yes. I know.

Here is my point. If you are going to get a job at a company, then make sure you have done (and become) who you want to be the minute you walk in the door because where you start is how you are perceived and it is harder to get recognized internally when you start at a lower position than it is to walk in where you want to be at.

If you start a blog, you are the founder. Be the CEO of something, anything, and have a story to tell the minute you walk in the door to get a job, build a business, or just build better relationships. Have something worth telling.

WHAT MATTERS?

THE PEOPLE IN OUR LIVES

STOP WORRYING ABOUT SHIT THAT DOESN'T MATTER.

33

"It's Getting Better All The Time," by Brooks and Dunn.

It's dark out... I really am lost. I am on a train heading Southbound.

It has almost been an entire day unplugged from technology and I am at peace. I would recommend to anyone who has never tried. Turn off the channels that don't matter and find peace and happiness in the simple things.

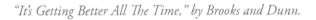

I could write an entire book on this. People spend so much time worrying about all the stuff, all the tedious details, all the problems that don't matter.

We spend our lives worrying about all of this stuff that doesn't really matter.

Some guy just fell down the stairs behind me so I just threw my computer down to help him. I am now rethinking those Jim Beams. :) Now I am distracted as hell. Just texted my mom back... Love ya.

Alright, focus damn it. What doesn't matter?

Your $100 shirt does not matter.
Your corvette does not matter.
Your hair does not matter.
Your makeup does not matter. (can't speak completely to that one but I love natural more anyways.)

My mom just wrote me "write your heart out..." I guess that is what you call it.

Your kitchen floor with a spec of dirt on it does not matter.
Your job title does not matter.
Your drunk facebook photo does not matter.
Your dirty shoe does not matter.
Your stain on your shirt does not matter.
Your job layoff does not matter.
Your broken cell phone does not matter.
Your camera you just lost does not matter.
Your friend that says you look dumb does not matter.
Your parter that just dumped you does not matter.
Your divorce does not matter.
Your ************* does not matter. (Fill it in.)

This list is endless. What matters? The people in our lives. I haven't bought a new piece of clothing *(I'm not a dirt bag... most of the time)* and I am happier than ever in my life.

The ability to say we can't go back and to know when something happens in life we can stop, adjust, and start from right now to make our life better. Next time you are worrying about something or when you find yourself in a down situation, relax for a second and realize that we create everything that happens to us, and only we can change what will happen in the future.

Work on realigning your path rather than dwelling on the past. All it will do is get you down for no reason. Why? It is not worth it... We have a short life to live on this earth so let's rock it now.

I'D RATHER HAVE SOMEONE THAT'S ALWAYS LEARNING THAN AN "EXPERT"

EXPERTS ARE MADE UP NAMES (EXCEPT MY DOCTOR).

34

"Summertime," by Kenny Chesney.

It's dark out, I just checked my cell phone but no signal... I really am lost. I am on a train heading Southbound still.

Music is amazing how it can lift you up, bring you down, and make you reflect on old times. I am thinking about the road. Airport road. My old buddies and I used to cruise it in Nick's Camaro just singing our ass off.

This one is going to be short. I am almost ten hours into this and loving every minute of it. Holy shit, does time fly when you are writing.

δ

I believe an expert can exist in fields that require a long time of study and are based around science, medicine, etc.

The problem is that nowadays there are experts everywhere and they are in fields such as Management, Social Media, Marketing, Business in general, and it goes on. Take it for what it is worth but

I run from these types of "experts." I think it shows arrogance and a sense of entitlement—and that is not who I want on my team. Would I have a beer with them? Hell yeah. I am not saying they are bad people at all, I am just saying that I would not want to do business with them. I stick with being an "amateur," who is learning as he goes.

RESUMES DON'T GET JOBS, BUT YOU STILL MAY NEED ONE.

35

"Old Blue Chair," by Kenny Chesney.

Back in my seat, no idea where we are. I am on a train heading Southbound stillllllllllll.

I just got bored so I snapped some head shots. Not very good... but what do I say? Why worry about it?

δ

Am I bashing resumes? No. If that is all you use to get a job, then good luck. I say you will have a job you don't like and be pissed off all day. Always work on the relationships and then when they ask, give them the resume. Screw online job boards too. Spend time finding companies you would want to work at, find the people in the positions that you would be working with and search out for their email, twitter, phone, anything.

Remember, don't go in the door asking... Go in the door inspiring.

If you find a name but no email then just use some clever trial and

IF A RESUME
IS ALL
YOU USE TO
GET A JOB

GOOD LUCK

error to introduce yourself and skip past HR. If the person's name is Shane Mac and he works at Company X there is a really good chance his email will be one of two things: *smac@companyx.com* or *shane@companyx.com.* Try them out. A quick introduction and how you found them and then just say you like what the company does and find something that the person you are contacting has been mentioned for before. Search google, newspapers, blogs, or try a tool called Gist that will show you everything about someone and allow you to have some info to congratulate them on. If you can tell them you have heard of them before and that is why you are contacting them then people will like you. That's how it works. People like to be praised. That's PR right? Just feature people who you want to feature you? That's the easiest way in the door. Don't be a scum bag though and have a legit interest in the person you are contacting.

(Did someone ask if I was writing a book? Kenny Chesney is on repeat and I have to change that. Love that guy but overload is no good.)

Anyways, back to resumes. Just focus on connecting with the right people, getting past HR, and make the introduction yourself to the people that matter. It is easier than you think. One other method. If you have to use a resume and cover letter, then think about making a business plan. It is actually simple and is usually less work than a cover letter but it just sets you apart and shows that you are thinking outside the box. Do a 30, 60, and 90 day business plan with 1 year goal that outlines what you want to get done and learn within that time period. If you want to see an example then email *bizplan@shanemac.me* and you will receive an auto-responder email with a link to the one I used to get the job offers I received. These were back during the out of college job offers and the business plan just helps you get in the door. What you have to say when you get there is the most important.

SAY
HELLO

IT'S THAT
SIMPLE

HI.

36

"When I think about leaving," by Kenny Chesney.

Back in my seat, no idea where we are. I am on a train heading Southbound. We spend much of our time complicating things and staring at our computer screens. What am I talking about? That's exactly what I am doing right now.

Just got distracted by the Consumer Safety instructions pamphlet. Darned.

δ

This is a true story. A friend of mine was complaining about hating their job and wanting to move up in the company. They said they busted their ass and did everything asked of them. I asked one simple question. Do you see the person who would promote you every single day? Their answer: No.

So I told them to try this: Everyday, walk by the person who would promote you and say hello... Every. Single. Day. They told me that they were on the fourth floor and I laughed... Who gives a shit? Get off Facebook for five minutes, take a break, and walk by their desk and say hello. That simple hello will spark a conversation after a while.

Needless to say, three weeks later that friend called me thanking me and saying I changed their life... Ha, I really didn't change their life but I just helped them realize that if people don't know who you are, what you do, and what you can offer then they can't promote you.

It all starts with Hi.

NEVER SAY NEVER.

37

"American Pie," by Don Mclean.

Back in my seat, no idea where we are. I am on a train heading Southbound.

δ

There is nothing else to say for this topic. Chapter done. I'm going to listen to this entire song of American Pie just because I love it. I think it is an 8 minute song so I will be back at 7:32 PM. Peace out for a minute and if you are reading this go listen to it. It rocks anytime.

Speaking of that, whiskey?

BOREDOM IS FAILURE

DIVERSITY BREEDS CONFIDENCE

JACK OF ALL TRADES, MASTER OF NONE.

38

"American Pie," by Don Mclean.

I wonder how everyone is doing? No contact besides a couple people all day is pretty crazy coming from a social crack addict like myself. It is awesome though.

δ

I get this all the time because I am a musician, biz guy, love trying new things, and creating a lot of different stuff. I agree with a blog post by Tim Ferriss on this argument.

Tim says five things which I totally agree with.

1. Specialists overestimate the time needed to 'master' a skill and confuse 'master' with 'perfect.'
2. In the world of dogmatic specialist it's the generalist who runs the show. (i.e. CEO, Founders, Biz Owners)
3. Boredom is Failure. I believe this more than ever. Lack of intellectual stimulation—not superlative material wealth—is what drives us to depression.

4. Diversity breeds confidence instead of fear of the unknown. The more you try new things and overcome the fear, the easier it will be to overcome the next challenge.

5. It's just more fun. It is the process of pursuing excellence that is exciting.

This is pretty much the business major. I believe that doing just one thing of anything will kill anyone's morale. I started hating music when I had to do it for a job every day. I played the same 40 songs night after night. I had to branch out. Change it up.

δ

O crap, that was the first yawn... and Joe Rogan's comedy skit just came on. This shit is hilarious. Taking a 10 minute break and sending a tweet. Just checked my word count and I have 15,000 words written today in about 10 hours. Alright, I'm back and loaded up with two more whiskeys. These will be the last ones of the night.

SOCIAL MEDIA IS OUR CHALKBOARD.

39

"Here I go again," by Whitesnake.

There is snow on the ground and we are climbing up an incline. Maybe the mountains in northern California? Who knows? All I know is Jim Bean and Diet and 5000 more words tonight.

δ

Social Media reminds me of Goodwill Hunting. It allows the low man on the totem pole to have a voice. It allows a starter position who has some knowledge to do something outside of their job title and get recognized by writing, recording, or speaking out in the channels that allow anyone to have a voice.

The opposite is also true. It allows everyone to see the CEO or the Executive Team is not as smart as they think they are. No one is there to write their speech for them, design all of their marketing emails, make them look smart. No one. Social Media is more like a leveling tool than anything else in the corporate arena. It allows anyone, in any role, at any time to get recognized. As long as you are not an idiot you should be fine.

DO THINGS TO INSPIRE OTHERS

CHARITY.
DO GOOD.

40

"Summer Nights," by Grease.

The shuffling of the cards next to me really makes me want to play some poker. The dad has a Canada jersey draped over him probably because they just whooped us Americans in the olympic championship for hockey.

δ

The shuffling of the cards next to me really makes me want to play some poker. The dad has a Canada jersey draped over him probably because they just whooped us Americans in the olympic championship for hockey.

As I write all of this book I stop for a second and think about where I am, what I am doing, and how amazing this experience is. (I can't stop smirking... Is that how you spell that spell checker?) I think about all of it and then think about a campaign I did over the past three months for my favorite non-profits called charity: water.

I am building a well in Africa and that is how all of this started. That is what sparked something in me to help others. The fact that communities in Africa don't even have clean drinking water and people die every day because of it and I sit here drinking whiskeys and water and soda. Like it doesn't matter. Sick. Disgusting. Makes me pissed. Angry. Sad. Why?

Wonder Why? I just don't get it. It is too big for me to comprehend but it just makes me really think about everything we think we "know." All of the jobs we NEED and all the stuff we NEED and all the bills we NEED and on and on and on and on and on. Our needs are a gross expectation that we believe we need because that expectation is created. I understand we want to have sanitation, a nice house, and the necessities, and it is not bad to have other stuff too. I am not saying that at all. I just think about the reality and it kind of makes me think. Think a lot.

You can set up a campaign at charity: water in under five minutes at *www.mycharitywater.org.* All you have to do is ask your friends to join you and make a campaign for anything that you want. Your birthday, parent's anniversary, dog's birthday, anything. It doesn't matter. It will be your campaign and you will see the actual well that you help build.

This can help you in careers as well by giving you something to point at when you talk to the HR, the manager, the person who will hire you. This is what I mean by doing things the inspire others. They will probably want to join in on your campaign and you should ask them too.

IT MAKES ME REALLY THINK ABOUT EVERYTHING WE THINK WE "KNOW"

THE LONGER YOU DWELL ON WHAT YOU CAN'T CHANGE THE HARDER IT WILL BE TO MOVE ON

YOU CONTROL
YOUR OWN
DESTINY.
NOT.

41

"Angels Like Her," by Trent Tomlinsin.

Three whiskeys down, one to go. Coming up on the 11 hour mark. Whoot whoot whoot. No, that was not a train whistle. That was my fist pump.

δ

I hear this all the time. You are in control of your own destiny. I don't agree completely. If you are an entrepreneur, a business owner, or even an employee at a company you could be in control but the truth is that many of us are not. Most of us work for someone else. Our employment is usually tied directly to whether or not a company is profitable. The minute they are not you are gone. Out of your control. You will look for another job and it will be the same situation. Can you work your way up in an organization and keep your job? Probably, but it still comes down to money. With that said I don't think you really do create your own destiny if you work for a company in the "corporate" or not so "corporate" world.

I believe it is up to you to make yourself the person they can't let go—but that doesn't always work either. Sometimes it is out of your control. Here is why I think the way I do:

I moved to Seattle for what I thought was a "dream job." I had a great job with a great company, but I never could have imagined what would happen three weeks after I moved there. I had just moved my entire life across the country to Seattle and three weeks after I start my job, half of my department was laid off. HOLY SHIT. I remember that moment. That day. That first take I caught of my boss that hired me who was getting laid off as well. How did my boss just get laid off? He just hired me. Why? How? Because I was cheaper... That is the only reason. That was the moment when I realized what had to be done. Relationships—not job titles—were the secret, and that's what I did.

So what can you do? Work your ass off and do the best at what you are given, but realize that if the bad thing happens and you feel like the job world isn't fair, just move on. Move on quickly. Without grudges. Without hate. Just move on and find your next path. The longer you dwell on what you can't change the harder it will be to move on and find the next great thing that is waiting for you. Move on. Always. Fast. Never burn a bridge. Ever. This world is small. Very small and that bridge will crumble you later if you burn it. Move on with Respect.

MANAGEMENT IS CREATED.

42

"Signs," by Tesla.

Yawn, yawn, yawn, drink, drink, drink... This may be the last post of the night. What an incredible day.

My writing is starting to slow down, that is for sure. My mind is starting to slow down and I'm not sure if it is the whiskey or it is the eleven-hour mark coming up. I just checked twitter again for the second time today. #addiction.

δ

Do we need leaders? Yes. Managers? I am not so sure. I mean there is an entire business college that is built around management, but really? I mean really? It is not some business function that has always existed. It is created. Is this a knock on managers? Not at all. It is just saying that we would be better off working in a collaborative state as a team rather than having managers. For the record, I have had great managers and it was not a problem. I just hear that so many people are getting micro-managed and there is nothing worse than that. If you feel like you are being micro-managed then buy them the book *Drive* by Dan Pink as a present. If that doesn't change their mind, then you are probably fighting a lost cause anyways.

No one wants to feel like they are being told what to do and they have no say in why they are doing it. There really is nothing worse than that.

"Billy's Got his Beer Goggles" on just came into the headphones. Maybe that is a sign? Shit, I don't know. I can't tell if it is the whiskey or this white screen that is making my head hurt. Either way, let's call it a night. Next topic will be tomorrow.

Goodnight.

Sleeping on a train tonight. San Francisco tomorrow.

NO ONE
WANTS TO FEEL
LIKE THEY ARE
BEING TOLD
WHAT TO DO

AND HAVE
NO SAY IN
WHY THEY
ARE DOING IT

6:22 AM

2:53 PM

SATURDAY

SAY
"THANK
YOU"
AND
"I'M SORRY"
OFTEN

THANK YOU.
I'M SORRY.

43

"Every Morning," by Sugar Ray.

Brush teeth, Starbucks (after brushed teeth... blah) and just talked to one of my best friends, Eric. Wooooooohoooooooo I feel good today.

δ

Thank you.

Such a simple phrase never to be forgotten. Whether you are on Social Media, at a coffee shop, or holding the door for a stranger. Thank you will get you further in life than any other one phrase. Thank you is the moment when people gain respect, crack a smile, or strike up a conversation. Use often and with purpose.

I'm Sorry.

Such a simple phrase, and it can be the hardest two words to say in our language. Our life. Our society. Instead of saying I'm sorry, recognizing your mistakes, and having an honest conversation that starts with "I'm Sorry," people instead spend their effort trying to find reasons, excuses, justifications to their actions and try to avoid this phrase.

Stop. Don't. Do. It. Anymore.

Face your mistakes, apologize, rebuild, rekindle. "I'm Sorry" with purpose and truth can rebuild more than any excuse you can come up with.

Remember this in life, careers, business, anything. Anything. Truly anything.

The train car is pitch black. A "no trespassing" sign lurks out my window to the right. I think it really means don't cross the tracks when train is coming. Not smart.

I am so stoked for today that I cannot even tell you. I plan to move around the city, meet new friends, and write some more from different spots around the city. I hope you are enjoying the ride so far.

9-5 NEEDS A LITTLE RETHINK MAYBE?

44

"Addicted," by Simple Plan.

Coffee Breath. Blah. Opened my blinds to let more light in, checked my phone, shut off phone. Back at it.

δ

Before you start thinking I am against 9-5, let me explain myself. Most people in the online world nowadays all have the same message... Screw 9-5. Not me. Not at all. Gathering like-minded people together between certain instances of time has great benefits in my mind. It allows for better collaboration, teamwork, and leadership. It also has its financial benefits with energy, supplies, etc.

Here is what I see as the problem: many people don't do their best work between 9-5. Many people would work better, more effectively, without arbitrary timeframes and instead with project guidelines. You have to have something done and you should get that done in the allotted time for the project.

MANY
PEOPLE
DON'T
DO THEIR
BEST WORK
BETWEEN
9-5

Example: my own story. I write and think more creatively between 6 AM and 9 AM than any other part of the day. By 2 PM I am usually an ADHD crack-dude and can't focus on anything longer than four seconds. So is it the concept of the day job that is bad? No, I don't think so. I just think people shouldn't be tied to a start time and end time arbitrarily. The psychology of 9-5 probably restricts more than one would think, and people may actually work better without that restriction. It really just pisses people off.

If you used Parkinsin's Law and said you have a day to get this done, then sometimes people may be done early and be happy to get out early while some days they may stay all night. When they are tied to the completion of a task or project rather than the clock on the wall, people feel invested in what they are doing which is important to employee happiness.

This topic might have just sucked and I am not really sure if it is worth being in this book but hey, that's the journey right?

I see some awesome mountains off to the right. The train is cruising along now and I turned on my phone for some reason. Turning back off. I have a serious problem. Addiction to this damn thing. I remember when all we had was a landline and the telemarketer would call around dinner time every night and we would always jump to answer it. 309-697-3976. That was it. My first number ever. I wonder if anyone has that now? Curious.

IF YOU FEEL
LIKE YOU
ARE STUCK
TRAPPED
LOST
THEN START
TALKING
ABOUT IT

FALLING IN TUNNELS. BLINDED.

45

"Home," by Edward Sharpe and the Magnetic Zeros.

Suburban America out my window and a song playing that reminds me of my brother, Max. My Dad. My Mom. My Sister. My Family.

δ

The problem is usually what we can't see or think we can't see. I have been there. Been blind. Felt like nothing else was out there, and didn't know where I wanted to go. Had to go. But where? How? When? When we start falling into these tunnels throughout our life we can easily get blinded by what is out there.

This happens at work. In relationships. Everywhere. We start doing something and even when we know it isn't right anymore or it is not what we want to do, we think we are trapped. The more unhappy and blinded we get the harder it is to see. It is a downward spiral. Down. Hard.

It takes a true friend. Someone to grab your ass and lift you up.

My brother. He was there. He was the voice, the person, the one who let me know what life was about. Much of this book and my opinions are influenced by his morals, values, and views on life.

If you feel like you are stuck, trapped, lost, then start talking about it. People will listen. Stop drinking your sorrows away and start communicating honestly. If that is too hard then get on the internet and find strangers that can let you know that so much more is out there. Waiting.

This world is so massive and there is too much that one can do. Seeing it is easier than you think if you know where to look. It is always funny looking back on where you were and what you thought you couldn't change yet it is so easy.

Go.

POLITICS ARE
LIKE GRADE
SCHOOL RECESS.

46

"I Want It That Way," by the Backstreet Boys.

Speaking of Grade School, how about some Backstreet Boys? What? The mountains are coming closer and the sun is coming up quickly. San Francisco is close.

δ

I spent my life listening to politics. Thinking about the two-party system. Trying to choose a side. Be part of the clique that it is.

Really? Why?

The truth is that politics confuse the shit out of me. The more I try to learn about it, the more I get confused. I listen to the quotes and read the writings of our founding fathers and I think to myself, "Is this what they were saying?" It sure doesn't seem that way.

Jack and Diane just came on... Ironic and time for a little ditty in the heartland.

Anyways, I look at our Republicans and Democrats and think about my days on the swing set. There were the cool kids and the losers. The problem is that both groups thought they were the cool kids. Nothing good ever came out of the split groups and it usually just caused problems. Our teachers would tell us to be leaders, think for ourselves, and when we voted in the classroom we had to put our heads down so we couldn't vote with our friends. It made sense. People, like it or not, feel obligated to stick with their friends—their party for that matter.

People always cheated. They always snuck a peek to make sure they were with their friends. Change never really happened. The majority always won because of belonging not believing. That is what I see. Today. Right now with Politics.

For someone to tell me that every Republican believes in every Republican initiative and every Democrat believes in every Democrat initiative—I would say you are full of shit, and until we start voting based on what we believe, not where we belong, I don't see much changing in our world of politics.

The problem is that the votes are not anonymous, and probably can't be for us voter's sake, so they will sit, scared, being the sissies that they are, hanging around in their two-party frat that it is. (Frats are not bad. I am not saying that. Frats are bad when they are running our country, and that is pretty much how I see it.)

Alright, that was a rant but something I believe strongly about. Sweet Caroline just came on... I think I am on my wedding mix and loving it. What a way to wake up. The view is starting to get amazing again. I wonder if I will roll into San Francisco past the Golden Gate Bridge. We shall find out soon...

I WOULD SAY: YOU ARE FULL OF SHIT

LEARN AS
YOU GO

LEARN BY
DOING

CREATING
SOMETHING IS
EXCITING

WHY IS SCHOOL BORING AS HELL?

47

"Sweet Caroline," by Neil Diamond.

Trailer Park out right and the feeling of serenity is making me sit here and smile. I still can't believe what has happened in my life over the past year. Where I am. What I am doing. Humbled as hell.

δ

I loved school. Mainly because I love people. Being around people. Talking. Man, do I talk a lot.

The school framework that I think back on, that I remember, was not stimulating. A few classes were, and I remember those. I remember what I learned. Why?

A lady just walked by and yelled at me because she read the title on my screen. Whoops.

Anyways, it is excitement and creating that really teaches and helps students retain information. I can think back to 3rd grade and sing every president because our Teacher, Ms. Huber at the time, taught us a song. She did everything a little different. She made it fun. I remember a lot from that class still to this day.

Here is the point: whether we should or can overhaul the school system is all based upon individual teachers' attitudes and how they go about teaching. It is more about what you do for yourself. Before, during, or after you are out of school. Keep learning and do so by creating solutions to problems. Learn as you go. Make it fun. Make it unique. Most importantly, create something so that when you are done, you have something to show for it. Create a book... :), a song, a picture, a design, a TV stand. It really doesn't matter, but learn by doing. Then re-do to get better.

MULTIPLE
STREAMS OF
INCOME.

48

"Since You've Been Gone," by Kelly Clarkson.

Just checked twitter and Matt Chevy says I am Insane. In a good way but Insane. Thanks Matt.

δ

Am I insane? Hell, who knows. Lately people have been telling me that I am living the un-templated lifestyle. I work a corporate job but I am also an entrepreneur. I call it a Corpreneur I guess. Came up with that name taking to Nate Rich, a buddy from Denver.

It really comes down to Multiple Streams of income. Most people work during the day and spend their money at night. They don't think they can do multiple jobs. That is crap. It is so easy nowadays to find something small, something so simple, that a lot of people could want. Open a store on *Shopify.com,* play guitar at the bar on Saturday nights, or help small companies in your area of 'expertise.' (Use that "expert" word sparingly.)

START DOING SOMETHING

SHANE MAC

It is just this mindset I see most of the time: that I will work during the day and I will wait for my raise to make more money. It isn't even about the money. The real thing to realize is that when you are working on a little project or product you are not spending money. I save so much money by doing things after my day job rather than going out every night, blowing all my money on booze with my friends, and never getting anywhere in your life financially. Always working for that next paycheck.

Music is awesome because you get paid to drink... it is rough... :)

The point here is to start something outside of your day job. Start helping out with something you know a little bit about. Learn. Grow. Do it more. Help out others. Start an online store with a product that you would be the first person to use. Start doing something. It is not about the next huge project. It is about something so small, so unique, so awesome that you believe in it and get excited to do it. That is when it is not work. It is life.

IT IS NOT REWARDING FOR ANYONE IF YOU ARE BORED AND NOT BUSY

WHO TOOK A SHIT TODAY?

49

"I Saw The Sign," by Ace of Base.

Awesomeness... I think this song is from Jock Jams Volume 3... Boom Boom Boom is next.

δ

I run meetings every day. I ask people a lot, "What are you working on?" If your face looks like I just asked you if you took a shit today, then you better tell me you are bored as hell and want to do something awesome. People are so scared of job security when they don't have enough to do at work that they are afraid to just say I DON'T HAVE ENOUGH TO DO. Instead they sit there and look like I asked them if they took a shit. It is not rewarding for anyone if you are bored and not busy. There is always something to do and you will be seen as a person with ambition if you would just be honest and say that you don't have enough to do.

This single thought of always letting people know when you don't have enough to do is the biggest factor in how I was able to get a voice within my last company. You get put on projects and teams that you would have otherwise not had the opportunity to join. You will learn. You will grow. Most importantly though, you will have a voice with a larger audience.

There is a sign out my window that says 34. Does that mean 34 miles to San Francisco? There is a ship yard out to the left and Backstreet Boys are back in the headphones... Back to Jock Jams... or maybe The Verve Pipe, "The Freshman."

YOU REALLY CAN DO ANYTHING.

50

"The Freshman," by The Verve Pipe.

δ

Thinking back on being a Freshman. At that time I was still in sports mode. I thought that was it. I went to college and got a major. I thought that was it. I got out and found a job. I thought that was it. I found another job. I thought that was it. Why do we always try to find the one thing that is 'IT?' Is there really the 'one?' The one job? The one person? The one path? I don't think so. I really don't know, though.

I think anyone that dedicates a certain amount of time, over time, to any scenario can achieve what they set out to do. This is within reason and realistic expectations. There are physical limitations and mental disabilities that can inhibit some, but besides that it just takes time.

Time. Focus over Time.

IT IS NOT
ABOUT BEING
THE BEST

BUT LEARNING
FROM IT

SO YOU CAN BE
WHERE
YOU WANT
TO BE

Do you think I became a musician over night? Hell no. I sucked. I sucked really bad. I learned to sing and I am still not great at it, but I just do it. I am not the best guitar player by any means but I just do it. I am not the best but I am sponsored by Miller Lite and was just awarded the Best Wedding Band in Seattle, WA.

Many people will say you have to be the BEST at something and that my advice is crap but I would disagree. I am FOR SURE not the best musician at all in Seattle. There are so many people in the world that the number of people who will be the best at something is almost nil. Even if you think you are the best you probably just have not come across the person who is actually better. It is not about being the best rather doing, and doing, and doing, and doing, and learning as you go, accepting criticism, and learning from it so you can be where you want to be.

The best thing to remember is that when you get there and you have put in all of that time, you will always have that skill but may just need a little brushing up to do sometime. You will never know what you truly love if you don't try. Next time you say no I suck at that just remember, almost everyone starts out by sucking at it. A rare few are "naturals."

WE CAN'T
FORESEE
WHAT WE
DON'T
KNOW

IT IS A
GAME

PLAY
IT

IT IS JUST A
GAME,
SO PLAY IT.
LIFE.

51

"A Drop In The Ocean," by Ron Pope.

The train hasn't moved in a few. I'm staring at a hill listening to a love song. This song is incredible. As I say that we start moving. Rolling. On our way again. Big ship Nordic Moon out the window. I don't think this is a river. A gentle woman's voice comes over the speaker. The diner car is open and serving breakfast. I might go grab a coffee after this one. I still can't believe I am doing this right now. Another ship... "The World Harmony." I wonder where they travel too. I think of that career. That life of a true shipmate. I am rolling my eyes thinking about how much a sissy I am typing on my computer...

δ

I don't mean "game" in a bad way. What I mean is that jobs, friends, attraction, everything in this life is just trial and error, learning from mistakes and successes, and trying again. Sometimes you will feel like you have won and other times you feel like you have lost.

The job you didn't get, the raise you didn't get, the friends that stabbed you in the back, the list goes on. The truth is that we need to adjust as we go. We can't foresee what we don't know. We try to plan our steps but forget to realize that what happens today will greatly affect tomorrow and what happens tomorrow will greatly affect the next day.

I think of it more as a main vision while practicing your day-to-day skills, so that when you are on deck you are ready when you step up to the plate. We will all have a few strikeouts in our life but with each strikeout comes a keener eye, a quicker turnaround time, and a stronger player in the game.

Are you playing life like a game and not letting the small setbacks stop you from jumping back in the game to try again? Start swinging and if you swing for the fence and miss then try bunting the next time. Either way you can still get on base.

I need some more coffee. Heading to the diner car and checking out until San Francisco. Next entry will be at a coffee shop most likely looking out over the Bay at Alcatraz. Good morning everyone.

TWO DAYS.
AMAZING PEOPLE.
ALL TWITTER.
BACK AT IT.

52

"Thunderstruck," by AC / DC.

δ

It's been a day and a half and I have met more great people in that short period of time than I could ever have imagined. It was incredible. Amazing. Simply mind blowing. Why? Twitter. Just another case study for you. As I sit here on the San Francisco Bay at The Water Front Bar and Grill and look at the sail boats coasting along in the amazing sunshine I stop. Smile. Glance at the bartender. Smile. She has no idea what I am writing. She just knows that I really wanted those Oyster Mushrooms. She is super nice and just gave me an awesome Jones Diet Soda. I have never had one but I would say you should try it. It rocks.

This trip was the trip I needed. The trip that slowed it all down. Got away. Relaxed. Met people that were only virtual before this. It is a weird feeling how the minute I meet them face to face I felt as if we had been friends for years. Forever. I truly believe the ability to read what people are writing, relate to someone, and discover people by watching them and going out of your way to meet them is more powerful than we all think. Every person I met last night is someone I would look to for advice, for inspiration, for guidance, for anything. They are incredible. Go and say hello now.

The mushrooms are here and man they look good. Time out.

Alright, I am signing out until the Train ride back to Seattle tonight. I have a ton more to write about and I am going to dive into tools, tips, and all the details on what and how I have gotten done in my life. Can't wait to share.

Signing out and going to play some guitar on the waterfront for a while.

Have a great day.

THE ABILITY TO DISCOVER PEOPLE

AND GO OUT OF YOUR WAY TO MEET THEM

IS MORE POWERFUL THAN WE ALL THINK

Sunday, March 7, 2010

11:33 AM

6:22 AM

THE RIDE BACK

NEVER TAKE "NO" IF YOU BELIEVE IN SOMETHING

RECEIVED
HIGHEST % RAISE
IN ONE YEAR.

53

"Love Shack" by The B-52's.

I made my own sleeper car last night. I am too damn big to sleep in the coach seat so I headed down to the diner car and slept in a booth. It was actually pretty dang comfortable. I am yawning like crazy and enjoying the awesome view out the left side of the train. Love shack in my headphones... not so much. Boooya, Green Grass Grows - Tim McGraw. Let's get this started right.

δ

From here on it will be instances that have happened in my life and while I feel fortunate and humbled for what has happened in my life, I do not share them to brag, boast, or to say I am better than anyone. I share with details, reasons, thoughts on "why" and "how" it happened so others can Kick Their Career's Ass.

After one year and 64 days working in what most would call a 'corporate job,' I received amazing news. I was getting an 8% raise. My boss busted her ass to get me that raise and after an awesome year with my team and a few innovative ideas getting implemented into action I was sure the other person on my team was getting an awesome raise as well.

Wrong. None. Nadda. Zip.

Actually, it wasn't just my partner in crime who was the "software brains" behind the concepts—no one around me was getting raises. Just me. What the F***? Really? No way? Was it my boss's fault? Not at all. So I stopped and thought about why me? What makes me get this incredible raise while my teammates didn't? I asked if I could split my raise with my team. No. Can't do that. I know I am no better than the sum of my parts. My Team, but here is why I think it happened...

Sitting outside the diner car makes me freaking hungry. Food. No Food. She loves me. She loves me not... ADDDDDDDDDDD

Really though, why me? Did I do a better job than everyone else? Up for debate but here is what I did do. My thoughts.

Everyone told me no when I asked if we could make the new product. No. We can't do that. I knew we could. I stayed late. Built it outside of work. Completed it. Presented it. Got my hand smacked and had to come in early to apologize for overstepping my boundaries. I should never do that again. But then we launched it, I believed in it, it worked better. I was recognized in the Senior Leadership meeting a month later. Why?

Never take NO if you believe in something enough.

Build friends with everyone. Everyone. Anyone. Care about what other people are working on. Care. Everyone you work with at the end of the day is part of a team. A bigger picture. All working together. People want to feel like the work they are doing is important, and the truth is, it is. Let them know that, meet new people, and make friends because you never know when that person you are befriending can help you down the road or when you can help them. It also allows you the chance to tell people what you do and what you like to do. Remember, if people don't know what you do they can't help you. Don't ever brag but let people know what you are working on.

This one is a true reflection that I don't agree with at all but I think plays a role. Extroverts get rewarded. This is not cool. Not cool at all. I know I talk a lot and am probably the biggest extrovert on earth. I love meeting people and hearing people's story, but why does the extrovert get rewarded? My partner in crime this entire year did not receive a dime yet he built everything with me. He might have done more work than me. Yet I get the raise? I am determined to change how this happens because I believe many great folks don't get rewarded from a trait that is irrelevant to job performance but do recognize it can make a difference.

Ask Questions. You already know that. Asking shows caring, learning, and starts discussions. Ask people at the top of your company. People you are "scared" to talk to. They are the same as you and they will ultimately be the person approving that raise. Make sure they know that name on the paper when it hits their desk. Remember that the question doesn't need to be anything about work. Just make them like you.

Work outside your job title. People like to think what they are doing is what they are the best at. They like to think that other people could not do what they do (most of the time). In business that is mostly a false statement. Business is problem solving.

Simple as that. Work to listen to what others are working on and when you see something that doesn't seem right or maybe could benefit from a tool or idea you have, make sure you let them know your thoughts. Instead of saying "I do it like this and I think you should do it like me," try phrasing it like this "We have had that problem before and I think I may have a tool that could help you do that quicker. Let me know if you have a minute and I would be happy to show you." If you are marketing, management, program management, a VP, or any other business job title, you can help out a lot more places than your job title describes. It will make you seem smart. Going above and beyond. Start small. Start by listening.

Leverage. I had a job offer and I let my boss know that I wasn't looking to leave, but this job landed in my lap. I was confused and I didn't know what to do. I wanted her guidance. Ask for help but let them know that others see value in you. A lot of value. Leverage. If done correctly, this is the single most powerful factor you can use to get a voice, get a raise, get noticed. IF.

IF.

IF. You have been doing great work already. Don't try this if you haven't done anything and want to just use a fake job offer to scare your employer because they will probably just tell you where the door is. You will know if people think you are doing good work. People will respect you and know what you are doing.

First step though: be good at what you do.

Right now, go reread that list. Think about each one and what can you do today. Right now. Write down an action, a small task for today, and get yourself an awesome raise this year.

BUSINESS
IS
PROBLEM
SOLVING

elp your career search.

B.S. here.

192

SHANE MAC

MORE THAN DOUBLED MY SALARY IN A YEAR.

54

"What Hurts The Most," by The Rascal Flatts.

My mind is a little scattered this morning. A little heavy for some reason. A little hungover and slept on a couch might be a reason for that. Out the window is flat land and a small two-lane road running parallel to the tracks. I am starting to think about the week ahead. The life change that I just made by quitting my job on Thursday of last week and heading to a new job Wednesday of this week. Excited as hell, but just thinking. Thankful mostly for what my last job presented me with... Options. Choices. Life.

δ

This one is easy: don't settle. It is easy for many of us to get a job and then stay content for three years. Then have a mid-career crisis, freak out, and start looking for another job or like many people they wait until they get laid off to start looking.

STOP.

The day you get hired you should look at what positions you would like to do. Start looking at other companies. Not for jobs, you have one of those. For the people who work around those jobs. Connect with them on a personal level. You have a job. You don't look like you want anything. Never mention jobs, careers, or even the job title you think you would like to have. Just make friends. When you have the opportunity to jump onto another train (job) it is much easier when the job calls you and you don't call the job. This is how you do it. The day you start the job you are in. It doesn't have to happen in a year but it is about building the channels to companies you would like to work for well in advance of ever wanting to work there. This method will also save your ass with your current employer who might fire you if you are looking for jobs.

Important note. Go for a job title you would like. Be good at. Enjoy. Money is not the object here, as I believe money is relative to what you buy, not who you are after a certain point. Ya, there is poverty and that would suck and I feel blessed that I am not there but after a certain level money is null and it is completely based on what you buy. That doesn't create happiness. It is Maslow's Hierarchy of needs that says it best:

"Lack of intellectual stimulation, not superlative material wealth, is what drives us to depression and emotional bankruptcy."

I believe boredom will kill dreams and jobs faster than anything else in life. Companies should focus Corporation on Community.

LACK OF INTELLECTUAL STIMULATION

NOT MATERIAL WEALTH

IS WHAT DRIVES US TO DEPRESSION

CHANGE
THIS
NOW

CHANGE HOMEPAGE TO BANK. SCREW YAHOO.

55

"Recovery," by Mer.

I am going to start diving into details. The day-to-day Shane Mac mind. Watch out because I am a nutcase and this could get crazy. Take each tip, tool, idea for what it is worth, but realize you do not have to be like me. Actually, you shouldn't be like me, but you could take some of the information and try it for yourself.

δ

I had Yahoo as the home page of my browser. I spent thirty minutes every morning reading about the top ten ways to text message girls and finding out that John Mayer said a cuss word in an interview. The site is like crack cocaine on the internet. Change. Change it now. Change your homepage to your bank. Why? Every day you will check your account and it will save you a ton of money (no joke). It only takes 2-3 minutes and then you decide what you need to do next. This ties into my next point.

Do this right now... Go ahead, I'll wait.

DON'T LET
CONTENT
COME TO YOU

ELIMINATE IT

BE YOUR
OWN RSS.

56

"I Saw The Sign," by Ace of Base.

Train is rolling through a nice little factory town and I am thinking about food. Why am I always hungry? Who cares because Ace of Base just came on... Awesome.

δ

I did it. I had Google Reader. I had 100 unread articles that I needed to read every day. I did it. I about died. I put a knife in Google Reader and life has never been better, and here is why:

1. Even though I liked the post that got me to subscribe to your blog or feed, that does not mean that every post is good or worth reading. (Including myself. It is just how it is.) I ended up reading a majority of posts that I would have never wanted to read if they weren't stuffed down my throat and made me feel guilty for not reading in my Google Reader or RSS feed.

2. Don't let content come to you. This is what kills most of us.

Everything is coming at us. We can't dodge it. You have to eliminate it. I am not saying you shouldn't keep a list of blogs you like to read or you shouldn't have an RSS folder of latest documents, I am just saying don't have it visually tell you that you have UNREAD posts to read. You will just waste your time filtering through what you probably wouldn't have wanted to read anyways.

If you love being a Consumption Whore then ignore this section. If not, delete your guilt-friendly RSS reader and make a list of URL's that you can search on your own time. Most of those blogs have a "best of" widget so you can focus on their best posts anyways or just search for what you really want to know.

MY THEORY ON A.D.H.D. AND A.D.D.

57

"Under the Bridge," by Rockapella (Red Hot Chili Peppers Cover).

Train came to a gentle stop. Small town America. Logging town it looks like. I wonder if the Gold Miner's lives were anything like what we live today. I wonder if any of them who made the journey westward actually made it rich in gold. That was only 160 years ago. Not that long ago really. Incredible that I never hear about gold anymore. Probably because it is the basis of our monetary system which is pretty scary considering the amount of paper money we are printing. Off topic... Focus. Focus on my theory on ADD... Ironic.

δ

I totally understand that there are chemical imbalances that occur in our brains, and they can cause a lot of different problems. A lot of different issues. A.D.H.D. being one of them. Lately though, I hear an astronomical amount of people that blame A.D.D. and A.D.H.D. for about everything. Anything. Here is my theory:

I believe that A.D.D., for most people, is just the overstimulation of an over-abundance of information. I believe that everyone has this problem. When too much information is coming at you, you can't consume it all. Can't process it. It turns into chaos. This isn't A.D.D., it is the channels and instantaneity of information that is a part of everyone's lives nowadays. Stop using this as an excuse for not executing and set up automatic filters. Close Email. Turn off your phone. Get rid of RSS. Get a notebook. Get off your computer.

Honestly, SLOW THE F*** DOWN. Trust me, it is hard. I have to focus on focusing. Not kidding. But when I eliminate these channels it makes it much easier. I am a hyper-crazy mind tank and I know that. Recognize the problems, eliminate the noise and start getting stuff done. Status updates and emails do not make products. They build relationships though so don't ignore them but just set time aside to do them. I tweet all day because it is my motivation and relationships through that channel that keep me going. Prioritize where you are getting value from.

SLOW THE FUCK DOWN

STATUS UPDATES AND EMAILS DO NOT MAKE PRODUCTS

USE A BUSINESS PLAN TO HELP YOUR CAREER SEARCH.

58

"Semi-Charmed Life," by Third Eye Blind.

I am starving and heading to the diner car. Time out. I'm Back. Just had breakfast with two nice ladies and a older gentleman. Three of us didn't talk (hard to believe I shut up for that long). One lady took the table by storm. She was trying to sell me on some weight loss drug that was going to make me feel better. Ha. Wrong guy for that. Anyways, snow is on the ground and back at it. Current Time: 9:19 AM.

δ

People always spend so much time doing things that offer so little value. People spend days... I mean days (I did too) on their resume and spend hours upon hours reworking their cover letter.

For what? A three-second glimpse at your cover letter and then under thirty seconds for your resume? This is not saying you don't need either of these tools (I just landed my new job without them ever seeing my resume by the way) but you need to recognize that you only have that amount of time and get creative with it. People say it all the time—"work smarter, not harder,"—and this is never more true than in this situation.

If you have three seconds in your email cover letter to catch your reader's attention, then what does your first line say? It better say something about them, not you. People like to be praised. Companies like to be praised. It is human nature.

What does your second line say? It better say something completely unique, inspiring, and/or valuable so that the reader will say to themselves ... I want to read more. If not, you are toast. This is where I used the business plan. It is actually super easy and does not take that much time. What it does is set you apart. It makes you stand out in a crowd of the same cover-letter-and-resume world we live in. FML. (F My Life for those who don't know.)

It is a 30, 60, 90 day goal plan (or list) of what you want to do within the company. What are you going to do for THEM. They can be super high-level. The idea here isn't that you have the answers to change the business, it is that you are willing to learn and dive right in when you get the chance. It is really about the person reading it saying to themselves, "I have never seen something like this before." (Once you get on the phone that is another story and I will address later.)

You can also throw in a one-year goal to show longevity.

If you would like to see exactly how I would approach an employer with an email and the business plan attached (the one I actually used to get interviews) send an email to *bizplan@shanemac.me* (already mentioned this) and you will receive an auto-responder that is exactly how I landed interviews. Simple, unique, and actually was effective for me.

THE E-REFERENCE LETTERS.

59

"Closing Time," by Third Eye Blind.

I sit listening to a couple guys next to me talking about drugs and their lives. They are talking about how they knew more than past employers. It is pretty ironic... ha. I smile, they just looked at me, and I snap a picture out the window. The train can make you a little dizzy if you sit facing backwards. I am right now for the first time. Getting all dizzy.

δ

All of us have had someone say something about us. Something that is worth remembering. You need those words. Here is what I did and it worked awesomely.

Instead of waiting until you need reference letters and asking past employers, teachers, or friends to write them, start now. Get it in an electronic version and ask the person if they would be fine if you changed the date and business name on it so you could use it for other companies. You need to emphasize that you are doing this so that it will save them time and you will never have to bug

ALL OF US
HAVE HAD
SOMEONE SAY
SOMETHING
ABOUT US
THAT IS
WORTH
REMEMBERING

them again. If you are really cool with them ask them if you can sign their signature if you have other jobs so they won't have to. They just have to be legit when they get called. DO NOT SIGN WITHOUT PERMISSION. If not, get a scanned image and use that. This gives you an awesome reference letter that you can personalize to every employer, anytime you want. This is a time saver and will be the foundation for your "Bad Ass Book," which I will talk about next.

If you would like to read a reference letter from out of college job hunting, I have a link in the email auto-responder that I set up above. Just email *bizplan@shanemac.me* and click on the reference letter link. Feel free to use my cover letter as a template and provide to your references so they really don't have to do much.

The secret to all of this is to give the employer what they want before they ask for it.

Make them say... "Well Damn, who is this fellow?"

It is like a white blanket outside. I didn't even realize it was snowing... Awesome. Time for Christmas music. :)

ARROGANCE
WILL
KILL YOU

I AM A
BAD ASS BOOK.

60

"Oops I Did It Again," by Britney Spears.

I think I did it again ...O Britney. It is snowing like a machine outside and is actually a pretty cool site with an entire train car of windows. I just realized I think I lost my flip video camera at the train stop in San Francisco. Not cool.

δ

First off, never repeat the title of this topic. Never say you are a bad ass. Arrogance will kill you. Just know that it is your bad ass book. Here is what I mean:

When you walk into the interview you want something to give to the people across the table. I recommend making 5 books for each interview. If they have more than that then they can share. Here is what I mean by the Bad Ass Book.

1. The book is just a nice black folder with a business card slot on the inside pocket. Buy a lot of these folders at your local drug store. CVS, Walgreens, or any department super store.

2. Business cards. This is just for perception and contact info. If you don't have any experience to put on the card just have your name and contact info. It is more of a nameplate for your folder with contact info. It is better to have no experience on it rather than some made up title you try to make. Many people nowadays would say business cards are irrelevant but I would disagree and say a tangible contact piece can have its place. Know when to use it. Will it hurt you not to have this piece? Probably not.

3. In the left pocket you want to put your business plan and your resume.

4. In the right pocket you will put your reference letters that are unique to this company and position.

5. Start passing them out when called upon to show your stuff. It will give you something to talk about. Go over the business plan, then dive into resume if you want, and then just make them aware of the letters and let them read at their leisure. Make people aware of what you did but don't cram it down their throat.

That's it. After you get your documents set up you can make these rather quickly. I used it to land my first couple of jobs and it worked great.

The lady from breakfast just stopped by and asked if she could have lunch with me because she said "I think I have more to learn from you." Ha. Should I spend 30 minutes talking with her because I feel bad if I don't? Decisions. Maybe I will want a break by then anyways. Who knows. Playing it by ear.

THE INTERVIEW.
NO BS HERE.

61

"Adam's Song," by Blink 182.

The guys next to me are talking about how the system is BS and they hate the stupid job they have. I am wondering should I say hello? Distractions. Time to put in the other headphone and focus. Focus.

δ

I hear so much interview advice it makes me sick. All this talk about having all the answers and knowing all the questions that the interviewer is going to ask... Blah, Blah, Blah. Screw all of it, in my opinion. If you focus on specific questions then you are just setting yourself up to be caught off guard and you will sit nervously waiting for the next question. I hated that. I did it. Sucked. I then read a section of "Pharmaceutical Bootcamp" a while back that talked about focusing on seven traits that every interview will be looking for. Works like a charm. Check it out.

They said to focus on these seven traits:

1. Leadership
2. Teamwork
3. Work Ethic
4. Integrity
5. Organization
6. Adaptability (resourcefulness)
7. Overcoming adversity, change, or failure

What I did to make this easy is picked three major events in my life to focus on. If you try to go in the interview with every idea from your life you will be overwhelmed. Focus. Think of your best job you had, a sports, music, or extracurricular activity that had challenges and failures, and then one more major part of life: could be academics.

You may stray from these three but if you think of the seven traits in each of these you will be able to tailor most of your answers to those specific instances. This should help with nerves and then you just have to wait for the crazy question as I call it. The "Sell me this pen," question or any other. Remember that it doesn't matter what the question is, it is about your process of doing it. The object at hand doesn't matter it is about the process of how you go about it. If it helps just envision it as something you would love to sell or do. Passion breeds confidence. Identify what the need is and work to find a solution. There are entire books written on this so my job here is done with that.

Holy cow we just stopped at the top of the Cascade mountains and the view is incredible. A massive lake, snow, and very, very tall evergreens. How the heck did Lewis and Clark walk all the way out here. We are such a sissy society now. Including me.

One more thing. In the interview, I get more respect and appreciation by being honest about what I don't know. YOU DON'T HAVE TO HAVE EVERY ANSWER AND YOU REALLY DON'T HAVE TO ALWAYS BE RIGHT. It is about your willingness to adapt and learn not "know it all" wisdom. Make that willingness apparent while also showing your knowledge and wisdom through stories and real situations that you have encountered in your life.

YOU GET MORE
RESPECT BY

BEING
HONEST
ABOUT WHAT
YOU DON'T
KNOW

GET TO THE RIGHT PEOPLE.

62

"One Song, Glory" by Rent Sountrack.

I'm already thinking about lunch and I just ate. Maybe I shouldn't sit by the door to the diner car.

δ

Many people nowadays are talking about video resumes. Video pitches. Video everything really. I haven't heard a great solution though so I set out to start a company for this exact reason.

I spent six months applying for jobs by sending a link to the person that I would be working for. I found them through the internet channels and would record a one minute video just saying hello. The secret was that it wasn't a page about me, it was a page labeled to them, about them.

Stop talking about yourself and start introducing yourself. The page was specific to the person and it had a simple text "hello" on the left and it said "push play" on the video of me on the right.

Basically, that was it. I had contact info directly below the video and I received calls at about an 80% rate. It worked. It was simple yet wasn't a video pitch. It shouldn't replace your resume because people need that tangible checklist. It is your way in the door because as much as we can deny it, the way you articulate, speak, look has a lot to do with the job search. This cuts out the bullshit and saves everyone time.

With that said, I have a start up, *http://sayhellothere.com,* so that anyone can make a unique page for every single job you are applying for. It is stupid simple and allows anyone to have all of their content in one place and a professional looking video intro to say hello.

HOW I
GET JOBS.

63

"Being Drunk's A Lot Like Loving You," by Kenny Chesney.

Another Amtrak comes speeding by the window. The sun is shining bright and a lake off to the left looks awesome to go jump in right now.

δ

This will be short. I actually just landed a job without ever sending my resume. Amazing job and I am stoked to get started.

What did I do?

I look at the job description and print it out. Go through every single bullet point and think about what you would do for the company for every single job description on the list. Do it. Now.

I was going to be doing email marketing, A/B testing, and homepage design/copy stuff. What did I do? I looked at what I was getting now and put together a deck of all of the ideas and thoughts I thought would be good to try.

I sent that over before I ever even mentioned the job. I didn't even mention that I had read the job description. I just did what they were looking for and gave it to them. The old "give before you get" mantra.

My first day is on Wednesday.

DO IT
NOW

BUSINESS IS ABOUT FINDING SOLUTIONS

SHANE MAC

THE BUSINESS DEGREE.

64

"She Don't Know She's Beautiful" by Kenny Chesney.

New topic going on next to me. I quote, "I don't think we should require people to go to high school." His argument is that not everyone can succeed. I am totally eavesdropping. They are talking about the repetition of school. Making valid points. I am going to get a soda.

δ

Before I write this, let me say that I have a degree in Business. Finance and Economics. I was marketing for two years until I started recognizing that 60% of my business college was marketing and I need to set myself apart.

I also believed, as I still do, that marketing and management are better learned through experience and trial and error whereas financials models and economic principles would be better learned in the classroom. Mainly though, my roommate, who took notes and told me when to go to class, was going to be a Finance and Economics major and I figured I could steal his notes. Ya, I was that guy. The D-bag that stole notes and now I swear by them.

Regardless of your major or focus in college though, Business is about finding solutions. Business is about the process of taking something to someone or vice versa. Unless you are going to be the mastermind behind some investment trading algorithm, I believe that any business major can do most business jobs. I feel like the system of college that makes us focus on a specific business major can sometimes limit us in our career search.

I understand the need to focus on a major and focus on a certain aspect of business to become the best at that area, but I feel like it can kill your job search. You limit your job search to that area when you could really do a number of other areas, and in my opinion, you would be qualified for. Then, they will teach you what you need to know based on your curiosity and critical thinking, which will determine your growth within that job.

LEARN THROUGH EXPERIENCE

ONCE YOU FIND
YOUR WAY IN
THE DOOR YOU
NEED
TO
HAVE
SOMETHING
TO
SAY

WHY I DID AN E-BOOK. HAVE SOMETHING TO SAY.

65

"Hit Me With Your Best Shot," by Joan Jett.

So the Cascade Mountains are incredible. The sun is coming out and the train car is coming alive. This trip has got me thinking a lot about family, friends, life, everything. I would recommend a train ride to anyone. Don't have a time limit though because they are not fast. We are cruising past a logging field at this very moment.

δ

Everyone is making an e-book it seems. I made one too. Why? I liked the simple topic of "If I would have known just one thing," but mostly I did it for a reason to contact and build relationships with people whose word I valued. It gave me a reason to walk in the door and something to talk about. That is the secret. Once you find your way in the door you need to have something to say. The e-book allowed me to do this. It gave me a reason to contact them. A reason to hear their story and build a relationship with them. Simple as that.

Yeah, I believe that the e-book will be a great read from some of the 40 most inspiring people who I look up to but that is not the main reason why I did it. How do you make an e-book? Simple.

1. Open up text document.
2. Change settings to 8in by 6in.
3. Pick a topic or title.
4. Write something that is worth people's time.
5. If collaborative, ask people to join you because you value their word.
6. Export as PDF.
7. Done.

This is something that even if you do it and no one reads it ... You did it. It gives you something to talk about in that interview. It gives you something to talk about when you meet people. You are an author. Authors write words, just some do it better than others. Remember that.

THE
ELIMINATOR
LIST.

66

"Dude Looks Like A Lady," by Aerosmith.

My battery is dying quickly. I need to head downstairs to the lounge again where they have outlets. I will try and start this list then head downstairs.

δ

Before I moved to Seattle I had it all. XBox, Wii, Cable, Dishwasher, Microwave, TV, etc, etc, etc... You get the point. Ya know, the necessities. Ha, was I wrong about necessities. It all started when my brother wouldn't split the cable bill with me for the TV. I was like, what a jerk. Our house didn't have a microwave or a dishwasher. (I thought the world was ending...) Then after a month I realized something. I didn't miss any of it. I actually loved it. I slowed down and made dinner. I didn't use so many dishes and just took time to do the dishes (most of the time... we have a war going on who does the dishes more but my argument is that I use one bowl versus my brother using 19 pots and pans... He is an awesome cook. Awesome but messy. Feel free to stop by for dinner anytime.)

Anyways, here is my list of eliminations in one year and the effect of each. I am not saying that you should eliminate all the stuff that I do, but just a list to show you what I have done:

1. TV - $200 on craigslist. Hundreds of hours of life back to do something. Quit being a consumption whore.
2. XBox - They are fun but you have to have control. They can burn four hours faster than you can blink. Ironically your eyes are watering like crazy because you don't blink. Surprised more people don't have seizures playing that thing.
3. Wii - Please read above.
4. Dishwasher - I would still like one of these but it is not bad.
5. Microwave - I learned a lot about food, how food works, and I tell you what... I will never use a microwave again. I slow down, eat less, and enjoy each meal a lot more because I take time to prepare it. Great diet plan for any of you looking for a place to start. Throw the microwave to the curb. People crack me up when they are like... WHAT?!?!? AHHHH HOW DO YOU COOK THINGS? I'm like really? Wow. An oven.
6. Email on cell phone.
7. RSS. (You should know how I feel about this.)
8. A service model company. M2volt.
9. Yahoo.
10. Driving a lot. (Trying to eliminate but not looking too easy.)
11. Car. About To Be Gone.
12. Twitter. Ha not. I lie. I am a tweet whore but the people I meet through it are phenomenal.

Alright, my eyes are starting to close and I am typing gibberish. If you could only see what I just deleted... Sheesh. Checking out for a minute

SHANE MAC

GET RID OF SHIT YOU DON'T REALLY NEED

3:47 PM

2:04 PM

BACK IN OREGON

WHAT IS HOLDING YOU BACK?

SHANE MAC

A LUNCH CAN CHANGE A LIFE.

67

"Two," by Ryan Adams.

Alright, time to crank! I have about 7 hours left and a lot more to say. We are coming down to the wire. Just had lunch with 3 people who were all unemployed. Wow did that lunch hit me hard. Train is driving through a trailer park.

δ

I sit. Listening. A man of Mexican decent sits next to me. He is heading North looking for construction work, while two older ladies, one an author and one an artist, talk about their love for art but their inability to make money doing it. Then me. Some young jerk with a job who feels so fortunate, even more so now, to be where I am. This is all about the man at the table since he was in his early forties and seemed upset about the past three years of his life.

Construction. That is all he knew. We got past that and started talking about what he loves. What he really liked to do. Took about three minutes and he said his main love is cooking. Authentic

Mexican. He cooks for entire family gatherings of over 150 people and everyone loves his food.

I asked him, "Would you want to be a chef?"

He said, "would love to."

"What is holding you back?" I asked.

"Fear," he said, and "I have been doing construction for twenty years but laid off the past three."

I started laughing as I sit here writing this book and thinking of who I would want to give this book to. I asked him if he would rather work for himself or work for a restaurant. He said himself. I said have you ever thought about having a little taco cart? Have you ever thought about going to that construction site where you worked to serve them all lunch?

Felt like I was playing the old sex drinking game "Have you ever?" He said no.

We talked for a good hour and I helped him lay out small steps to try it out without taking massive risks and betting the farm on it. I told him to get a simple, small, niche recipe and try one day a week for a start. I went over the steps to start a business. From taxes, licensing, and risks involved.

We ended with a check list. A mental vision of what and where this was going to go. Most importantly, we ended with a simple test plan.

I am not about risking it all and following the live your dream stuff we hear every day. I believe in creating small, agile, efficient businesses that can test, learn, and adapt quickly to grow effectively.

As I parted to head back to my seat and finish this book I couldn't help but be humbled by what had just happened. A genuine man with two kids, a wife, a passion for being a cook, and the perfect opportunity to try it.

Will he try it? I gave him my contact info and I passed along contact info of people who I thought could help him around his area. I will contact him over the next couple weeks to keep him going. It was a great lunch at that.

Back to work.

"WHENEVER YOU
FIND
YOURSELF ON
THE SIDE OF
THE MAJORITY IT
IS TIME TO PAUSE
AND REFLECT"

-MARK TWAIN

401K
CONFUSES ME.

68

"There Are Places I Remember," by the Beatles.

As we roll into Salem, I start to think about the project that I am working on. The book that lies in my hands. In my computer, actually. I am starting to smile just thinking of how much I want to share this with my friends. My family. Everyone. If just one topic can help one person, then that is success to me. I know that everyone will not agree completely with all of my thoughts, and that is perfect. I hope people think critically about everything that I have said in this book. That is it. I want people to just think. Think a little bit differently. Maybe not even differently, just critically. If it is not working, fix it. That's all. On to a rant here about money stuff.

δ

Oh, the 401K. If you want to know the facts about this go to Wikipedia. Here is what I don't understand.

Ahhhh I have to turn off my phone... Distraction. Done.

So a system was created to pool money together so that we would have sustainable and above-average returns on our life savings for retirement. I am pretty sure the 401K system wasn't actually supposed to be a retirement system at all. It was pitched to companies and it somehow caught on and spread like wildfire.

Is having a retirement savings plan bad? Not at all! Here is what doesn't make sense to me:

Almost every company (a lot of people) contribute to the funds that make up the 401K. A LOT OF FREAKING MONEY. Who controls it? Not you. Not me. Some small group of people called "traders" (ironic) who have a piece of every person's life in their hands sitting on Wall Street trying to beat the market (system) to make a buck.

Temporary vision with long-term money. That's all.

I am taking my money and working with Financial people so that I can diversify my savings and get myself out of the majority. Mark Twain said it best, "Whenever you find yourself on the side of the majority it is time to pause and reflect."

This doesn't mean go jump off a bridge and do something crazy. It just means reflect and think about what you are doing.

Really, at the pace of the U.S. dollar inflation and debt in relation to other world currencies and financial markets, I wouldn't bet out the collapse of the U.S. Financial System. I know, I know, you are sitting there going HAHAHA YEAH right... We are America. We run this shit.

Did you know that the Federal Reserve is our third Central Bank? It is only around 100 years old and two have already failed. Look at the methods that cause financial collapses and stop listening to the message coming out of the megaphone called Washington.

I am not trying to be some crazy conspiracy person at all, but just thinking about the amount of debt that America has and the moment that a few countries want to cash in their U.S. money, it could hurt a little bit... Ouch.

RELIGION IS A PROBLEM WHEN IT PROMOTES NOT ACCEPTING DIFFERENCES

SHANE MAC

RELIGION CONFUSES ME MORE.

69

"Paradise Dashboard," by Meatloaf.

A woman sits to my right looking out the window staring at an empty pasture. We have never made eye contact on this entire trip sitting directly next to each other. All good though. She does have a bag of Chex Mix that I would love to snag... Man, do those sound great.

δ

Religion. This will be short because I see way too many people try to influence their opinion of religion on others. Me? Not so much. Here is the moment that changed my view and made me really confused until this day.

Two years ago I had a meeting. An afternoon meeting that lasted 4 or 5 hours where everyone got to present. Here is the lineup:

Me - White Boy Midwestern Wide Framed Half Hick Christian.

An Iranian - Awesome well-dressed Middle Eastern man who was Muslim.

An Iraqi - Larger framed man who was also a Muslim.

A Chinese Woman - A small cute Chinese woman not sure about her religion.

A Russian - A strong-spoken Russian man who wanted world peace. Not a Christian.

An Argentinean - A man who lived with respect and talked about a religion that I had never heard of.

A guy from India - One of my great friends and taught me a ton about India religion and culture.

The meeting is irrelevant. It was one moment at the end of the meeting when I said, "Awesome meeting today everyone, let's go grab some beers!" All agreed, gave high fives, and out the door we went. I stopped. Confused. Lost.

I think all of them are smart, inspiring, and awesome teammates. But we are all different religions? We are all different then? That moment is when I took the stance that we are all the same and I have no idea what I am, where I am going, or how I am going to get there. I will do my best to help, learn, and bring together people as people and forego the walls of religion that were built in my brain as a child. Religion promotes good things most of the time, but the only problem is when it promotes not accepting differences and then bad things happen.

I will stay confused and continue to study religion and learn about the history and origins of many of the powerful religions of the world.

Here's to One World. One. Person. At. A. Time.

WE ARE ALL THE SAME

AND I HAVE NO IDEA WHAT I AM WHERE I AM GOING OR HOW I AM GOING TO GET THERE

WE NEED
CREATIVITY
AND CRITICAL
THINKING

WE NEED
COLLABORATION

THE LECTURER DEATH.

70

"We Are The Champions," by Queen.

I think Portland is close and with that I feel the end of this book coming. I feel this incredible excitement about sharing this book, this story, these thoughts with people. I just had to pick up all of my stuff and move train cars because they are leaving the caboose in Portland. Took an extra 30 minutes. This trip home is a little more distracting than the trip down. All good though.

δ

Teachers. Speakers. Lecturing Professors. They are exactly what this new model of collaboration and internet is against. It is one person shouting to an audience of listeners. It inhibits collaboration and creativity. It is the industrial model. A bunch of cogs in the machine just listening to the person on stage.

Why?

This is the biggest problem in the classroom. We need creativity and critical thinking. We need collaboration. That is how we learn and solve problems. When a teacher, like a boss, tells you what, how, and why you need to do things we all lose our sense of leadership and creativity.

I find that in my life it is more about guiding people to start thinking critically and helping them see where to start. At my last company, we changed the word corporate to community.

We have to challenge each other. Disagree to find the right answers. Collaborate and realize that one person on the stage doesn't have all the right answers or solutions.

We need a conference that is a roundtable, a conference where people question the speaker, a classroom where the students help teach the teachers.

We all talk about the changing business model and the open communication channels and the new way of working together.

WE CAN ALL LEARN FROM EACH OTHER.

NO ONE HAS ALL THE ANSWERS.

NO ONE.

ANYWHERE.

EVER.

Alright that was a rant. Rant over.

WE CAN ALL LEARN FROM EACH OTHER

Sunday, March 7, 2010

7:40 PM

5:07 PM

BACK IN WASHINGTON

WE LIVE IN A DIFFERENT WORLD

MEMORIZING, SAT, ACT'S ARE DUMB NOWADAYS.

71

"You Belong With Me," by Taylor Swift.

Train just stopped and two cute blonde girls just started striking up conversation with me. I think it could be the two bottles of wine on the table. They seem nice but I am trying to stay focused here. I have drunk about ten Pepsi One's and I don't think I will ever drink this crap again. It tastes like poison right now. Ah.

δ

We live in a different world. We don't have to waste time on the task, details, and other time drains that we used to. We can focus on the strategies, creativity, and critical thinking that we really need to create a better educational and business system. As far as the ACT and SAT tests go, why do we spend our time cramming and memorizing and trying to brag about our scores—that I am better than others. I aced math yet you aced English. I am better than you. This mentality is the exact problem with corporate America. Arrogance along with Ignorance is the worst combination one can have.

I read a post about this the other day from Jeff Jarvis where he talked about testing and a new way to go about it. In his post he says, "Instead of giving tests to find out what they've [students] learned, we should test to find out what they don't know. Their wrong answers aren't failures, they are needs and opportunities."

This resonated strongly with me thinking about college, jobs, and business in general. We test and try to find who knows the most about something but forget to find out what people don't know and then educate them. That is the secret in my book. There is too much that we don't know to focus on the small piece of what we do.

Always remember this quote by Einstein, "Imagination is more important than knowledge."

IMAGINATION IS MORE IMPORTANT THAN KNOWLEDGE

DON'T BASH
SOMETHING IF
YOU ARE NOT
WILLING TO TRY
TO FIX IT

CHANGE CORPORATE TO COMMUNITY

72

"F*** Her Gently," by Tenacious D.

Another beautiful lake lies out the right window. Damn it, I just realized I am sitting backwards again. This makes me dizzy as hell. Whatever, moving on.

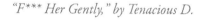

If you know me at all you know that I don't hate the "day job." I don't play in the "live-your-dream-anywhere-in-the-world" hype. I think you can if you are smart and want to, but the truth is that many people don't. Instead, I think that corporate gets a bad rap because it is not a community. Corporate is exactly what we have been talking about. It is the hierarchy's of scale where people at the top think they are smarter than people at the bottom.

Instead of bashing "corporate" or bashing "the 9-5," why not try to make it better? Why not work to change the word "corporate" to "community." I did it at my last company. I worked to open the lines of communication and help the leaders of our company realize that we can all learn from each other. Instead of bashing a system, why not strive to fix it? Make it better. It will give you the voice you wanted within your company and help you get a voice with the right people.

Show them articles about office hours, about collaboration. Don't bash something if you are not willing to try and fix it. Next time you say "screw this," or "this is so dumb." Stop. Think. Plan. Find a way to fix it and you will really find yourself with a credible voice. Always offer up a solution if you are going to tell someone they have a problem.

WHO DO I
LISTEN TO?

73

"All Right Now," by Bad Company.

I am so damn excited right now and just sitting here as I approach the 30,000 word mark which was that number in my head that I thought was a good goal and just stoked. Excited. Humbled. I don't even know really. If no one reads this book I don't care because it was an incredible experience to get this all out. On paper. A journey, nonetheless. Your Love just came on by the outfield... That is awesome... "Josie's on a vacation far away!"

δ

As this trip comes to an end I wanted to take a minute to make a list of all of those people, teammates, guides, inspirations who have gotten me to where I am today. I think anyone can benefit from listening to any of them. They all have a piece in this book becoming a reality. Thank you.

Many of them don't even know it: Dad, Mom, Brother, Sister, Hank Wasiak, Beth Andrus, Brett Byrd, Patrick Antrim, Tamee

Gunnell, Jim Keenan, Jason Fried, Sharalyn Hartwel, Penelope Trunk, Andrew Swenson, T.A. McCann, Jonathan Fields, My Hometown Boys and Girls, Tim Ferriss.

WHAT HAVE I CHECKED OFF THE LIST?

74

"Write This Down," by George Straight.

That's it. The last post. A book. I believe in. A total of over 30,000 words and I used to complain about 3 weeks to write under 3000. It is amazing what you can do when you set out to do it. You really can do anything and I am no better than anyone who will read this book. It is just about doing it. Call me an author all you want but it is just words on paper. Have you ever done that before? :) ... I thank you.

δ

I have a "kicking life's ass list" to keep a tab of what I have done in my life so far. Now I can add to it "2010--I wrote a book." I keep it to keep tabs on what I am doing. I still have so much more to get done. I have only just begun. You can do anything that you set out to do and it really is about doing.

END

CLOSING.

75

"Time Of Your Life," by Green Day.

δ

I really didn't think this day would happen. I really never even thought about writing a book. I have nothing left to say but...

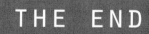

THE END

SHANE MAC

WELL, ALMOST THE
END.
OFF THE TRAIN.

SHANE MAC

LIFE.
IS.
A.
SECRET.
GAME.

76

"Unanswered Prayers," by Garth Brooks.

δ

I lay here on this morning listening to unanswered prayers and someone just commented on a blog post I wrote a while back and I thought why not have a bonus topic thrown in here a week later? So, here ya go. I throw in a blog post...

I sit.

Thinking. Smiling. Reflecting. Wondering...

About all of the people, the moments, the times that have changed my life. How did my path lead to where I am? Why do I feel so fortunate for everything that I have? Why am I typing and smiling so cheesy that the coffee shop barista probably thinks I am in love with this crack box called a computer?

Because it is incredible, but realize, it is a game.

A game of inspiring and enabling others. A game of doing the unexpected. That's it. The UNEXPECTED. Many of us do what is asked of us. That's not a bad thing per say. Imagine if we all didn't do what was asked of us? We try to Crush it in our jobs, in life, in everything for that matter. I look around and there are so many people that are all trying to do this one thing. Live. Enjoy. Create. Build. Better. But are we? Do you spend time at your job working on your tasks at hand or trying to bring everyone together to do more? Do you tell your boss that you have great ideas and they might help? Do you call your family and just say hi? Do you do things in your life that are not EXPECTED?

That. One. Thing. Is. The. Secret. Do what is not expected. Always.

If you have a girlfriend, heck with Valentine's Day and pick a different one. If you know someone's birthday is coming up, be the first to call... three days early. Same with holidays. Most of all (since a lot of us spend half of our awake life working) if you have a job, don't focus on your checklist in front of you. Make sure to get it done but start doing the unexpected. Think about your company as a whole and how you think other departments, other roles, other people, could benefit from something that you use, you know, you built. Think about the small things. Do you use a checklist that helps people? Anything. Think. You probably wait to speak up when you have your 'review.' Ya? Why? Why not ask for 15 minutes after work and make your own review or your own I HAVE AN IDEA talk. Chances are that you are already doing it. Just not in the unexpected way. People don't expect help. They think they should have to ask. That is crap. Everyone can use a hand. Realize that the expected only gets you the expected outcome. Also realize that this is always changing, evolving, and that the unexpected today will be expected tomorrow. Seth Godin said it recently in a blog post where he talked about a situation where the waitress remembered everything he ordered. He said:

"The first time someone does this to you in conversation (no matter how subtly), you're going to be blown away and flabbergasted. The tenth time, it'll be ordinary, and the 20th, boring."

So are you going for that 10% raise, the next job title, and more tasks with your new checklist or are you striving to do more? Are you trying to climb the ladder we all try to climb in the corporate world that just leads to another ladder? You must know and realize that there is no top of the ladder. Ever. It is just a climb to another ladder. Is that bad? No. Not at all. Just realize that it is not the cloud you think it is. The secret is about doing small things, the little things, the things in life that can catapult you to another level in everything you do. And guess what? It only takes... nothing. No. More. Effort. No. More. Time. Just. A. Different. Approach.

So tomorrow, head out to make someone smile, call an old friend, or let your boss know you think you can help. Never tell, just provide questions that make one think. Enable others to feel like they were able to see what they didn't know existed. Just ask. Why doesn't this work? Maybe this could work better? Why are you telling me happy birthday three days early? Because you care. Simple. You have to care though and if you don't then this post is useless. Worthless. Crap. By doing these simple things you will start to get noticed, get a voice, be seen as a leader. It is such a game of being heard and if nobody knows what you are thinking then you will sit there checking the box. Feeling like you can be more. You should be the CEO. You are better than this. The truth is, you are. Not that everyone should be a CEO but we should all feel like we can be something more... and we can. It is just easy to get caught in the routine and feel like no one is listening. Speak up. Now. Right now. If you get fired because you are trying to help then awesome… you don't want to work there. At all. Start doing what others wouldn't expect. You could spend your life working 9-5 checking off a list or you can start doing the unexpected. You can work 9-5 checking a list AND do the unexpected.

I am not some guy saying screw work and 9-5 is dumb. I am saying that you can kick your career's ass by doing things a little differently. A little unexpectedly (is that a word?). The unexpected is not crazy, it is appreciative. It is not jumping off a cliff, but rather climbing a new wall. It is not a golden ticket rather the tunnel from Shawshank Redemption. It takes time, takes humbleness, takes persistence, takes you believing in what you are doing so much that you will spend 15 years chipping away at a wall to build it. You are building a better life in this case instead of a tunnel to freedom. But that is it. You are already doing the stuff that I am talking about. The problem is that you are doing it like everyone else. You think Andy was the only person thinking about getting out of prison? Stop. Do the unexpected and kick ass in all you do from this day forward. Starting Now. Ask yourself, am I doing anything unexpected? Thoughts anyone? Am I talking crazy here?

UPDATE: I wrote this on Saturday, Feb. 6th, 2010 and at around noon my Dad showed up on our doorstep all the way from Illinois. Just bought a ticket and came to see his son's play some music as "The Son's of Theo." The unexpected, when done in great ways, is incredible and it was amazing to see my Dad.

DO THE
UNEXPECTED
AND KICK ASS
IN ALL THAT YOU
DO FROM THIS
DAY FORWARD

STARTING NOW

(THE END)

HELLO

SHANE MAC is the Director of Product for *Zaarly*, a local marketplace where you can work with amazing people to do just about anything. Since launching in 2011, Zaarly has been featured on the cover of *Entrepreneur* magazine and was ranked one of the 50 Most Innovative Companies by *Fast Company* in 2012. Prior to working at Zaarly, he helped build Gist, which was later sold for millions to Blackberry; founded *Hello There*, a new way to introduce yourself to people through an online platform, and started his career building products at Cobalt Group which was later acquired by ADP. He has been interviewed and featured on the *Wall Street Journal, New York Times, Reuters, USA Today*, while also speaking regularly for universities and companies on entrepreneurship and businesses. Silly fact: his wedding band was also voted the best in Seattle in 2009. Learn more or contact Shane at *http://shanemac.me/*

δ

START PUBLISHING

SAN FRANCISCO